ALWAYS BE BRAVE

JUSTIN R. RYAN, LPC

BALBOA.PRESS
A DIVISION OF HAY HOUSE

Balboa Press books may be ordered through booksellers or by contacting:

Balboa Press
A Division of Hay House
1663 Liberty Drive
Bloomington, IN 47403
www.balboapress.com
844-682-1282

Because of the dynamic nature of the Internet, any web addresses or links contained in this book may have changed since publication and may no longer be valid. The views expressed in this work are solely those of the author and do not necessarily reflect the views of the publisher, and the publisher hereby disclaims any responsibility for them.

The author of this book does not dispense medical advice or prescribe the use of any technique as a form of treatment for physical, emotional, or medical problems without the advice of a physician, either directly or indirectly. The intent of the author is only to offer information of a general nature to help you in your quest for emotional and spiritual well-being. In the event you use any of the information in this book for yourself, which is your constitutional right, the author and the publisher assume no responsibility for your actions.

Any people depicted in stock imagery provided by Getty Images are models, and such images are being used for illustrative purposes only. Certain stock imagery © Getty Images.

Print information available on the last page.

ISBN: 978-1-9822-5228-1 (sc)
ISBN: 978-1-9822-5229-8 (e)

Balboa Press rev. date: 09/25/2020

DEDICATION

THIS BOOK IS dedicated to my late father Quay Ryan. I spent the first part of my life doing everything I possibly could to not be like you, and now I take great comfort knowing that I am you.

CONTENTS

ACKNOWLEDGMENT

THERE IS A community of people I would like to thank, but first and foremost I want to praise God for all the gifts in my life. From family, to friends, to colleagues and peers, God has blessed me beyond belief. To my wife Cami, you mean everything to me. Thank you for always being by my side through thick and thin. I am deeply grateful for your enduring love and support. Next to my two boys, Talon and Chase. Whatever happens in life, I want you to "Always Be Brave," and follow your dreams. Take risks in life, reach for the stars, and know that your mother and I will be with you every step of the way. I am so proud of the both of you and love being your dad. I cannot wait to see what life has instore for you. Thank you also to my family especially my mother for their lifetime of love and encouragement.

To my supervisor and mentor Will Bishop. I think about you often and cannot thank you enough for the guidance and impact you have had in my life both on a personal and professional level. I can still remember when I first met you as a scared intern at DFI. We met in your office and went over my history, and also the fears and concerns I had about starting this journey. It was your belief in me first as a new therapist, and then later as a first time dad that made me who I am today. I owe you a lifetime of gratitude. Thank you.

Lastly, to the many friends and neighbors that I couldn't

possibly mention all by name. I am truly appreciative and indebted to all the love, generosity, and support that you have shown me and my family. I am so very grateful that my kids will grow up in a community surrounded by people who care for them, who they can trust and rely on, and who will guide and help shape their development. It truly does take a village and I'm so thankful that my kids have a village of people in place who love them unconditionally.

INTRO

EVER THOUGHT TO yourself, "man things would be so much better if I could live another person's life?" You see everyone around you living this happy, go lucky life, and think to yourself, "I wonder what it must feel like to have the perfect family, drive an expensive car, and not have a worry in the world?" Whether we want to admit it or not we have all done this in some sort of fashion during our life. We imagine what it must feel like to have more money, to be in better shape, and in general not feel so shitty about ourselves. We tell ourselves everything will be fine. We listen to self-help experts, download podcasts, and do exactly what we're told to do and try and be grateful for the things we have. Yet despite all this we still struggle to find inner happiness. When things get really bad, we even go back to basics and try to remind ourselves of those famous one-line statements that we see on bumper stickers or T-shirts. Ever heard these sayings, "if life gives you lemons make lemonade," or "nothing is impossible?" Growing up my mom would famously tell me "this too shall pass." Well sorry mom, but forget that.

The pain and hurt we feel on a daily basis is real. We're in debt, we're depressed, and not to mention the majority of us hate our job (I'll get to that later in this book). We struggle with weight and self-esteem issues, abuse and dependence are only getting worse, and the prescription pain epidemic has now become a societal problem. Had enough? Sorry there's more. There's also the deeper pain and trauma that causes us to go to very dark and dangerous places. There's the deeper pain that for years we have tried to repress and not think about.

The point here is that most of us carry a level of pain and hurt that is very real and emotional. Before we go any further let's try and make some agreements and compromise with each other.

First, let's try and agree to not compare each other's hurt and pain. Let's try and not have the mindset that what I went through is much worse and therefore you should just get over it. I call it the "Deadpool" syndrome. If you have ever seen the movie, "Deadpool," you know exactly what I'm talking about. If you haven't seen the movie let me explain. The two main characters in the movie have a scene where they start to compare whose life is worse. One person describes something really painful and traumatic that happened to them and then the other person tries to one up that. You experienced that, well I experienced this, and therefore I had it worse than you. For the purpose of this book, let's agree to not do this. On some level I sincerely believe that we all probably do this and tell ourselves "whatever I'm going through right now, or whatever I've experienced I know that other people have had it worse." There is nothing wrong with this type of mentality and we need to be able to empathize and show more compassion towards other people (I'll talk about this in later chapters so stay tuned). It's also healthy for us to acknowledge our own pain and suffering and ultimately want to get better. This doesn't mean that you're less compassionate or a bad person, it just means that you're going through a lot right now. In fact, I would argue that if you want to change your marriage, or change your family, or even change society for that matter, then you first need to work on yourself. So let's agree to not compare our pain and suffering, but instead try and heal ourselves, and get through this thing called life together.

Next, there is no magic pill in life. What I want this book to be for you is a step towards self-fulfillment. I fully understand

and accept that when you read this book not everything I say or recommend will be for you. Life is not a one size fits all, and certainly not as easy as a 1, 2, 3 step solution. What works for me may not work for you, and what works for you may not work for me. However, what I do want you to do is try and keep an open mind. You're going to read this book and start trying different things. You'll see what works and see what doesn't. You'll determine what's useful and what's not and then you'll read another book and do the exact same thing. Essentially, I want you to build your own toolbox and find things that you can use that will bring you inner peace and happiness.

Lastly, I want you to know my own history, not because this is a success story or anything like that, because trust me it's not. I want you to know about me because throughout this book I'm going to talk about my life including my family. First, I was adopted at 6 months of age from Korea. If this was 15 years ago and I was writing this same book I would probably keep this part out. Even as an adult I still struggle to openly talk about my adoption and how it has impacted my life and my personal relationships. If you haven't guessed yet, I'm also a therapist. When I was about 13 years old my parents were worried about my behavior and also concerned that I wasn't dealing with my adoption appropriately so instead of letting me figure this out on my own they rushed me off to therapy.

Ever see the movie "Good Will Hunting?" The story of the angry boy who was severely abused, raised in foster homes, and who would protect himself by not allowing other people to get close to him. However, underneath all of his anger was this highly intelligent genius just waiting to come out. Well, that's my life in a nutshell. After I went to therapy I was able to work through all the anger, embarrassment, and resentment I had about being adopted. I was able to find peace with being left at a train station by my birth mother and was able to work through feelings of abandonment and loss. I now live in a million dollar home and drive a Tesla. Yep my life is perfect. OK, so of course I'm lying. So this is what really happened.

As a kid I wouldn't talk to the therapist and ultimately refused to keep going. When I was about 20 years old, I went back to therapy and even met with that same therapist who I refused to talk to as an adolescent. I say this to you because what often happens in life is that even when we sort through all of the bullshit what ends up coming up is just more pain and confusion.

Socialists argue that there is only one degree of separation that divides us from each other. We all want the same thing in life. We all want to be healthy and happy, and when this doesn't happen we all feel the same confusion and disappointment. My argument here is that what separates those who are truly happy from those who are struggling is only one degree of separation. Does it help to have stability both as an adult and even more as a child? Yes, certainly. In fact, you probably won't find anyone who would be willing to argue that point.

Attachment and bonding are a critical piece of development, but does that mean you can't find true happiness and success if you grew up in less than ideal circumstances? No, it doesn't, and in fact I'll even bring up examples later in this book of people who were able to find success despite having to go through less than ideal circumstances. So if I experience emotions such as self-doubt, insecurity, and anxiety than my guess is that there are more people like me than there are not. Part of the process of change requires you to be comfortable within your own skin and be able to find your inner voice. For me this process took over 30 years of my life.

By writing this book my quest was to determine how to find inner peace and happiness. In my household whenever our kids are nervous, or scared, or just unsure of themselves, my wife and I always remind them of our family motto "Always Be Brave." Everything that I'm suggesting are things that I have to remind myself to do on a daily basis. I have compiled a list of ideas and concepts that I have used in my practice to help clients not only improve their lives and find deeper meaning, but also help them have deeper connection with their family and loved ones. Life is hard and change can be scary, but whether we know it or not we all have the inner ability to change. Yes, having money and being in shape helps, but I believe that the majority of us just want to be happy with who we are. All we want is to be proud of the person who is staring back at us when we look in a mirror. This book is broken down into very specific steps designed to give you certain assignments and tasks to implement into your daily life. Sound good? OK let's begin.

CHAPTER 1
GOAL SETTING

READ ANY THERAPY book whether it's a self-help book, how to improve your marriage, or even a parenting book, and most likely there will be a section on goal setting. This book is no different. Most therapists spend a significant amount of time with their clients having them identify goals that they would like to work on in therapy. In my practice, I usually have clients identify both short term goals within the session and also long term goals as well.

Establishing goals helps us to have direction, stay on track, and also holds us accountable. Furthermore, goal setting also increases our self-esteem and self-worth. Just think about this for a second. If you're a parent and make a promise to your kid that if they have a great week, you'll celebrate this achievement by getting ice cream at the end of the week. Your kid then ends up working hard throughout the entire week, and just like you promised on Friday you go out and get ice cream. Imagine how proud your child must feel in the moment eating ice cream while celebrating their accomplishment. It's the same thing with adults. Working towards achieving our goals and feeling the success of hard work will only increase our self-esteem and improve our self-confidence. The fact is according to Leslie Riopel, "setting goals helps trigger new behavior, helps guides your focus and helps you sustain that momentum in life" (Riopel, 2020). Now back to goals. My encouragement to you is to think about goal setting in three different steps.

Step #1- identify what you want. Before you can succeed, you first need to decide what you really want. Sounds simple right? Identify what you want, set it as a goal, and get after it. Let's try and simplify this even more. First, throughout the goal setting process let's start to use "I statements." I want _____, now you fill in the blank. "I statements," not only holds us accountable to complete our goals, but also empowers us along the way. Second, focus on one goal at a time. In no way am I suggesting that you shouldn't have multiple goals for yourself, because we all have different things in our lives that we want to accomplish. If you can balance multiple things at the same time and multi-task different priorities then maybe you can and should set multiple goals for yourself. If however, you're like me and you get overwhelmed and anxious with too many different things on your plate then I would suggest that you slow down and take one thing at a time. In addition, if you think of yourself as a system and if you change one part of that system then other things are bound to change as well. For example, if you want to get healthier and if you start to increase your exercise level other things within your system will change as well including your sleep, mood, and your motivation. The point here is before you do anything else go back to basics and determine what you want, and set it as a goal.

Step #2, Develop a Roadmap

OK, so you've made this great goal and have finally decided that now is the time that you are going to put everything behind you and find happiness. Good for you that you have taken this important step and decided that now is the time to put yourself first. OK great so now what? Step 2 involves coming up with a game plan. The way I describe step number 2, is to imagine a scale and that your main goal is point F on this scale. However, you can't get to point F without first starting at point A and then going through points B, C, D, and E that follow.

Imagine for a second that you made a goal to climb a mountain. You thought about this now for the past several years, but could never find the right time to do this until now. The first thing you do is go out and buy the right equipment (point A). You get new hiking shoes, a new backpack, and of course a stainless steel water bottle. The next day you wake up and drive to the bottom of the mountain (point B). You put on sunscreen and change into your new hiking shoes to protect yourself from the tough terrain that you are about to face. After you tighten your shoes and put on sunscreen you then start your hike (point C). The scenery is beautiful, the air is fresh and clean, but as you're walking up a steep hill you suddenly slip and hurt your knee. Luckily, you prepared for this and instead of turning around you brush the dirt and debris off your body and put a band aid over your cut (point D). Now comes the hard part. As the climb gets steeper and more dangerous you think to yourself, "well at least I'm almost done." You make it over a steep hill thinking that you've reached the top only to find that you're only half way there. Ask any climber one of the more challenging parts of climbing a mountain is when you realize you have been hiking for well over an hour and you are nowhere close to the top. Every part of you feels tired, sore, and defeated. You even think to yourself "I did pretty good maybe I should just stop for the day and try again next week" (point E). To me this is when we give up.

Ever made a New Year's resolution? Of course you have. Typically, people stay committed to their New Year's goal for maybe a month, two at the most, but then life happens. We start to feel dissuaded and overwhelmed, and end up forgetting about our New Year's resolution. Whatever goal you have, point E will happen. Life will get in the way and you'll start to doubt yourself and lose motivation and maybe even start to procrastinate. Take some deep breaths, tell yourself that you can do this, and start putting one foot in the front of the other until you get to the peak of your mountain (point F). Imagine what it must feel like to get to the top of your mountain. How much pride and accomplishment you would feel as you're looking out over a majestic scenery. We all want to get to the top of our mountain. Whether it is to be happy, get healthier, or even go back to school you first need to develop an action plan as to how to accomplish your goal.

Step number 3, figure out potential roadblocks

I have always believed that in order to have success you will need to identify potential roadblocks. In fact, this might not only be the most important step, but if you don't identify potential roadblocks this is where a lot of people get stuck and ultimately give up on their goals. Think about this for a second. Imagine for a second that you want to get a new job. You update your resume, get your cover letter together, have your list of references, and practice for the upcoming job interview. You rehearse every possible question and go over every possible scenario so that you are not only ready to go, but you are overly prepared for whatever comes your way. It's the same thing with goal setting. This step is a two-part process.

First, if you want to change your life figure out the potential roadblocks that might get in your way. Whatever your goal is there are bound to be things that will get in your way. While there are some roadblocks that you will be able to foresee (family, friends, self-motivation) there will also be other unpredictable life events that will unfortunately just happen (illness, loss of job, death of a loved one). For now, try and focus on the predictable roadblocks and try to control what you can control. Let this be the time that you finally achieve a goal from start to finish. Figuring out potential roadblocks will be a huge part of this process. I have always believed that one of the keys to recovery is having internal insight. Knowing who you are, what you want, and what your struggles are. My encouragement to you is to look inwards and figure out what are the things that are preventing you from accomplishing your goals.

Most of us use navigation when we drive. Navigation will warn us about potential hazardous conditions on the road, and will tell us when to turn, and will also let us know whether the destination is on the left- or right-hand side of the street. Most importantly, navigation will tell us if we're lost and will guide us as to how to get back on track. It's the same principal with goal setting. We need to have an internal navigation system in place to warn us when we are getting off track, or when we are about to encounter hazardous conditions. Finally, we also need an internal navigation system that will help us get to our goals, and also allow us to know when we have safely arrived at our final destination.

Step number 2- develop a plan as to how to go through potential obstacles. So you want to be happier, but you know you struggle with self-motivation. OK, so now develop a plan as to how you are going to hold yourself accountable. If you know self-motivation is something that is not one of your strengths, then develop a plan as to how you will hold yourself accountable. Are you going to make a daily checklist of things you need to get done? Or are you going to ask a trusted friend or family member for help? Whatever the case may be your challenge will be to get ahead of potential roadblocks and not allow these to prevent you from accomplishing your goal. Now let's put it all together. See diagram 1A.

1A

Step 1. Identify what you want

    I want to _____

Step 2. Develop a roadmap

    This is how I will meet my goal

    Point A. _____

    Point B. _____

    Point C. _____

    Point D. _____

Step 3- Identify Potential Roadblocks

    Potential Roadblock #1 _____

        Plan to overcome roadblock #1

            Step 1 _____

            Step 2 _____

    Potential Roadblock #2 _____

        Plan to overcome roadblock #2

            Step 1 _____

            Step 2 _____

CHAPTER 2
TAKING RISK

EVER THOUGHT TO yourself this is the week, or this is the month, or better yet this is the year that I start doing blank? I start losing weight, I start saving money, I start putting myself first, or I start dating other people. Whatever the blank is for you ever thought to yourself "why do I never follow through on the goals that I set for myself?" Or better yet the even harder question "what's wrong with me?"

There are many reasons why we struggle to meet our personal goals. We procrastinate, we give up, we move on, we doubt ourselves, and simply put shit just happens.

I would argue that instead of asking, "why do I feel stuck," we instead should be asking ourselves, "what separates those who take risk in life from those who don't?" OK, so let's clear the air and agree that for most people taking risk in life can be very scary. Whether it's speaking up during a team meeting, asking someone out on a date, or picking up a new hobby, all of these examples have one major thing in common. It's hard to put yourself out there. It is much easier and safer to avoid taking risk in life, instead of facing the possibility of rejection.

In fact, it is scientific evidence that our brains and our systems are designed for self-preservation. Our system warns us if there is danger, and protects us from harm. If we see danger in front us, our system says to us "run you dumbshit." Fight, flight, or flee, that's how our brain protects us. It's the same thing with taking risks. Our system is designed to protect us from hurtful emotions such as rejection, shame, and embarrassment. So for most of us things like taking risks in life are easier said than done.

For the most part our personalities are set in place at a very young age. Yes we grow and mature along the way, but in general we are who we are. For example, if growing up I'm a shy kid, then most likely I'll be an introvert as an adult. If I'm more comfortable as a kid being more reserved and introspective, do you really think I can change as an adult and start being the life of the party? Probably not, but what I do believe is regardless of your personality and comfort zone we can all start to learn how to take more risk in life.

The general feedback I get when people first meet me is that I come across as being guarded and somewhat unapproachable. Truth be told this is probably true. Nevertheless, what I can do is take the risk and present myself the way I want other people to see me as being humble, graceful, and thoughtful. So let's go back to what separates those who take risk and put themselves out there as opposed to those who don't. Yes they are absolutely confident and secure in themselves, and maybe even a little arrogant as well. What else? What really separates those who are willing to take risk in life from those who don't? My quest for this chapter was to really figure this out. Life is all about taking risk and exposing yourself to new situations. It's like a cycle, you try new things, you build new confidence, or you avoid taking risks in life and you remain feeling stuck. Well what happens if you fail? I'll get to that, trust me. Let's start from the beginning and talk about ways how you can start taking risks.

Get Your Ass out on the dance Floor

I call lesson number 1, "Get your ass out on the dance floor." For the most part we have all been in this type of scenario. Either you are at a bar with some friends, or at a wedding and then all of the sudden the music starts playing. Your anxiety immediately starts to rise, but instead of panicking you buy yourself some time as you move away from the dance area without anyone noticing. Up until that moment you were having a great time talking and laughing with friends, but now the night has turned into a full blown dance party. So what do you do? Most people start pounding more drinks because they know at some point they are eventually going to have to dance. Most of us are much more comfortable watching other people dance as opposed to being the first ones out on the dance floor. I have always believed that in this type of scenario there are five groups of people.

Person #1, the prototypical good dancer. These people have been blessed beyond belief with skill and talent that most of us do not possess. These people have no such problem getting the dance party started. If this is you, then count your lucky stars because everyone in the bar wishes they were you. Trust me on that. Shout out to my boy Cody Lancaster, who is not only an incredible dancer, but even a better person. When person number 1, starts to dance the entire place just sits back and watches in amazement.

Then there is person #2. This is the drunk/obnoxious guy at the bar who just repels everyone around them. This person is not only loud and does stupid things, but when this person moves out on the dance floor the entire crowd moves away from this person. We've all seen this guy. At first they think they're funny and try to dance with various people. Sometimes there's confrontation with other people, but most of the time people just think to themselves, "what a douchebag." If you are person number 2, take the risk and don't be this guy anymore. If we were honest with ourselves, my guess is that most guys have acted like person number 2 at least a few times in their mid-twenties. Regrettably, I know I have, and pray to God that my kids will do better than me and never follow in their dad's footsteps.

There's also person number 3. I describe these people as statue like figures. When the music starts playing they become statues and you just can't move them. I'm thinking of you Shannon Marotz. Their friends try and get them out on the dance floor, but eventually give up because doing something like this is just like trying to move a statue, you just can't do it.

Then there's person #4. If you're like me you definitely fall into this category. This person is much more comfortable watching other people dance, but might go out on the dance floor depending on how much alcohol is in our system. The mere thought of possibly having to dance causes instant anxiety. The inner secret that people number 4 have, is that we want to have fun, and we want to get out there and dance, but we don't have enough self-confidence to just get out there.

Finally, there's person #5. I would categorize this person as having some dance moves, but nothing like person number 1. The thing that separates this person from person number 3 and 4, is that when it comes to taking risk in life i.e. going out on the dance floor, these people do so with the mentality that they do not care what other people think about them. Why? Because they have the inner confidence in themselves and are proud of who they are. Ever been at a bar and seen a group of people just having fun and dancing with each other? Most likely, these people are group number 5's. Recently, my wife and I went out with a couple of our friends on a much needed parent's night out. We started the night out by hanging out and getting dinner, but ended the night at a bar with a dance floor. Now again, I'm in the category of person number 4. I have my strengths and I have my weaknesses, and dancing is definitely not one of my strengths. What I observed that night is my wife and some of the other moms out on the dance floor just having fun and not caring what other people thought of them (Person number 5). When my wife finally dragged me out on the dance floor the only thing I could of, was what were other people thinking about me? Were they laughing at me, or are they wondering why this beautiful woman was with such an uncoordinated douche? If you are like me (person 4), you think about this not only that night, but also the next morning. If you are like person 5 (my wife), you don't care what other people think. You had a great time, you enjoyed other people's company, and the next morning you don't think to yourself "I hope other people weren't laughing at me," but instead you think to yourself, "I had a really good night."

The point here is that again life is all about taking risk. Our challenge is to find the courage and get our ass out on the dance floor. Ever been in class and wanted to ask your teacher a question, but didn't because you thought other people would think that that question was stupid? Get your ass out on the dance floor. Ever been in a work meeting and had a really good idea, but instead of saying something you instead stayed quiet? Take the risk, and get out on the dance floor. If right now you're playing on a sports team, next time your coach asks for a volunteer to go first, find the courage and get out on the dance floor.

Learn how to fail

Lesson #2, Learn how to fail. Our society is based on evolution. We change, we grow, we evolve, we adapt, and yes we even fail. The good news is that despite our shortcomings, and despite our failures we continue to try and we continue to fight whether we know it or not. The hard thing here is that the message we start receiving at a young age is "failure is not an option." Remember, Ricky Bobby in "Talladega Nights," "if you're not first you're last." From a young age we are pushed to succeed and to win at all cost. Of course, nobody wants to fail. Nobody wants to feel embarrassed, or feel like they disappointed themselves or their family, but I would argue that failing is part of our development. If what prevents you from taking risk in life is the feeling of failure then there's no judgement from me. However, failing in life is not only part of our growth, but I would argue that some of the most successful people in sports, media, and business have not only failed, but failed miserably throughout their development.

Want an example? Michael Jordan got cut from his 9th grade basketball team, only to later win six NBA championships and become regarded as the greatest basketball player in NBA history. Before starting Microsoft, and becoming one of the richest people in the world, Bill Gates was the owner of a failed business company. So what can we take away and learn from really successful people? What do they have that we can really learn from? Are they confident, skilled, and talented? Yes. Did they have to work really hard and not give up? Yes, of course they did. What else? What do they have that we can learn from?

I believe that all successful people have an ability to self-reflect and learn from their failures. Not only do successful people take risks, but when they fail they have the insight to look inwards and learn from their mistakes. Wanna be a good parent, or have a successful marriage? Then you have to have a level of self-reflection. What did I do wrong, what do I need to do differently, and what do I need to change. Self-reflection equals success.

There are many reasons why we don't succeed in life, or why a marriage fails. But if we don't look at ourselves and ask ourselves "what did I do wrong," then we are bound to keep making the same mistakes over and over again. OK, so I know what you must be thinking right now. Success has nothing to do with self-reflection. In fact, success only happens if you're really smart, or if you catch a lucky break or two along the way. OK, so let's try and do this and agree that maybe both of us are right. Yes, it doesn't hurt to be super smart, but I would also note that some of the most successful people in the world didn't even finish college. Do this experiment and Google "successful people who dropped out of college." The top three on the list might be the three richest people in the world.

You're also probably right that more than a few successful people most likely caught a break or two along the way. But what about the successfully people who didn't catch a break? What about the other half who were raised in chaotic and less than ideal situations and had to work their way to the top? Research their stories and it's crystal clear that not only did they not catch a break, but at times it probably seemed that the world was against them.

See billionaire John Paul DeJoria, founder of John Paul Mitchell products, who was raised in the foster care system, was homeless at one point in his life, only later to become a billionaire entrepreneur (Pierre-Bravo, 2017). Want another example? We all know Oprah Winfrey and what she has accomplished in her life. From being a world renowned talk show host, to creating her own television network and magazine company, to now having an estimated network of 3 billion dollars (Elkins, 2015). What you might not know is that Oprah was born into poverty, subjected to sexual and physical abuse, and lost her infant son two weeks after his birth (Sackey, 2017).

If you really did do a Google search as previously mentioned, of "successful people who dropped out of college," you would find Oprah's name on that list. The point here is that success is what we make of it. If we only believe that in order to find success we have to come from a wealthy family, or attend a prestigious university then only a very few of us will ever find success. The reality is that most of us don't come from a wealthy family, and as such we have to make our own success. Most of our parents emphasized the value and importance of hard work and responsibility. Be proud of that, but also embrace failure. Challenge yourself and start thinking about what you need to do differently this next time in order to have success. Self-reflection equals success. You don't think Bill Gates after having a failed business had to ask himself some really hard questions and make some serious changes before he started his other company? If he didn't do that then my guess is that Microsoft would have failed just like his previous company.

We all want to succeed in life, but part of having success requires you to take risks with the possibility of failing. I know it's hard and can be very scary at times, but if we can learn from our mistakes and allow ourselves to grow from our failures then I truly believe you'll find success.

See the Good in other People

One of the things that I really love about my wife is that she is able to see the best in other people. Her mentality is that she gives everyone a chance, and focuses on their positives. I really love and respect this about her, but at the same time it drives me crazy. Often my response to her in real time is that she needs to live in the real world. Grudgingly, I have to admit she is right. If we are to really change and start taking risk in life, then we have to change our mentality and understand that the majority of people in this world are good in nature. We have to believe that the majority of people are considerate, thoughtful, and kind-hearted.

Are there bad people in this world? Of course there are. Ever seen "The Trials of Gabriel Fernandez," on Netflix? Holy shit there are bad people in this world. Are there people that are deceitful, greedy, and evil? Unfortunately, yes. Even worse, there are also people that have done very bad things and have violated trust in unthinkable ways. If this has happened to you I am truly sorry for the pain and confusion that other people have caused you. I am not suggesting in any way or in any fashion that you find the good in those people. What I am suggesting, and what I do believe is that those people are the minority. The majority of people, are people of good will.

I have had clients come in my office who have gone through unimaginable pain and unthinkable heartache. Their strength is courageous, and their will to get better and start trusting people again is truly inspiring. There is hope, and recovery is possible. My encouragement for you is to take the risk and seek help. Get an EMDR trained therapist and start your journey towards healing and fulfillment.

Now back to seeing the good in people. I will fully admit that this will be a really hard process for a lot of us including myself particularly in this current political climate. If we were to be honest with ourselves we already have these pre-conceived notions about other people based on our past experiences. We label people and put them in boxes based on how they look, how they act, how they parent, their political party, their sexual orientation, and who they worship. It's gotten so bad nowadays that we judge people on their patriotism, and whether or not they're American enough. The good news is that I believe the majority of us want our culture to change for the better. We want to move past all of this hatred and violence that consumes our society, and instead move towards equality and tolerance. However, if we want our society to change than we have to change with it. We can't expect our society to change if we don't start seeing the positives in other people.

Ever heard the saying we are more alike than different? Sure you have. We all experience the same emotions, have the same fears, and have the same concerns. Some of us more than others. Sadly, there are people right now who are facing real economic uncertainty. Do they need government solutions? Yes of course they do. They need real answers and real solutions right now. They're livelihoods are on the line. However, you know what they don't need? They don't need us to judge them. If right now you and your family are financial stable, that's great and you should be proud of that. But why look down on other people who aren't in your exact position, and think that they are any less than you? They are trying to provide for their family, just like you. We are more alike than we are different.

Here's another example. Remember, the parents night out I just mentioned, well earlier in the night I had an encounter with another guy who I determined was disrespecting me, and targeting me because of my skin color. Let me play out the scenario for you. I was standing by myself at the end of the bar waiting to get my wife a drink when a group of people sat down right next to where I was standing. OK fine, but then some guy decided to position himself between me and a girl who was sitting in the chair right next to me thus crowding my space. At the time I took this as a sign of disrespect and as an insult. What you think you can just crowd my space and do whatever you want too because you're white and I'm not. So what did I just do? I saw what I wanted to see in this other guy. He's of a different race than me and therefore, he thinks he is superior and can do whatever he wants and try to push me out of the way.

So what could I have done differently? Could I have seen the good in him? In the moment probably not, but what I could have done is slowed myself down and realized a couple of things. First, this guy probably just wants to stand next to his girlfriend. There's nothing wrong with that right? It was Saturday night, and he probably just wanted to be next to his girlfriend. Yes, he crowded my personal space, but he didn't touch me. In fact, we were in such a small area that he actually did a good job of trying to be next to his partner while at the same time trying to not invade my personal space.

Secondly, I could have done something different and been more empathic towards him and realized that he and I might have a lot in common. Let me explain. Ever been in a situation where the person you are with suddenly starts talking with someone else? You come out of the bathroom and think to yourself what happened? Before I went in everything was fine, and now the person who I was talking too, is now laughing and talking with someone else. I know that this has happened to me more times than I would like to remember. What if this guy saw me as a threat and before his girlfriend and I could even get the chance to say one word to each other, he decides to get ahead of it and cut it off. I know this sounds very ego-centric of me to say, but what if I'm right? What if his past experiences told him to be on alert that night and don't let something like this happen again? Well than what that means this guy and I are more alike than we are different. If we are truly going to change and start taking risk, it starts by being more empathic towards one another.

Lastly, I could have realized what was really going on with me. That week my oldest son was in his second week of kindergarten and as a family we were still struggling with drop off. That entire week was very emotional for me, and when this happened it just put me over the edge. So whose fault was it then? Was it this guy's fault that for the past two weeks my kid had been struggling with the transition to kindergarten? No. OK, so was it his fault that I had been an emotional wreck for the past two weeks? No. Well if it wasn't his fault than whose fault was it? That entire scenario was on me. Looking back I know I need to be better than that. I want a better world for my kids. The thought of them inheriting such a divided and hateful society scares me to my core. The truth of the matter is that in that scenario the only thing I did was add to a culture of hate and intolerance as opposed to being part of the solution. We all have to be better than that. I have to be better than that.

Stop Comparing Yourself

Lesson #4, Stop comparing yourself. The thing about comparing yourself to other people is that you are always bound to lose at this game. There will always be other people that are better looking than you, make more money, have a bigger home, and are in better shape. There's nothing wrong with challenging yourself and wanting more out of life, but if you are constantly comparing your life with what you do and don't have you'll never be able to find true happiness. For a lot us including myself this will be one of the harder challenges we face.

To be jealous and envies of other people is human nature. Back in the day, wars were started and countries were founded because one guy was jealous of what another guy had, so than that guy decided to go to war with that other guy, and then ended up stealing that other guy's land and while he was at it took his wife as well. The thing about the guy who goes around taking other people's castles and other people's wives is that they always end up wanting more. This is what ultimately leads to their demise.

We all get jealous, but at the same time we can use our jealously as self-motivation as opposed to letting our jealously tear ourselves and other people down. Will this be hard? Yes this will be extremely hard. Our culture not only promotes division, but encourages this superiority complex. The thing about this is that if you believe the only way for you to be truly happy is to have external things you'll never find true happiness (point #1). There will always be something more that you want and then something more after that. You'll tell yourself all I need is a bigger home to be truly happy. When that happens and you get a new home, you'll then tell yourself "OK what I really need is a new car and then after that my life will be set." Now getting a new car and a new home does help, but that probably only last for a couple of months, maybe even a year before you start to think to yourself "what I really need is a new RV."

Point number 2, again our society promotes division and a superiority complex. We separate people based on class, gender, race, and sexual orientation. We also separate people based on possessions. I have this; you don't so therefore I'm better than you. You get a new car; your friend sees that and then gets a new boat. After your friend gets a new boat, you then try to show your friend up by remodeling your home. You friend than responds by going out and buying a new mountain cabin. I have this, and you don't therefore, my life is better than yours. I'm not suggesting that you shouldn't want to remodel your home or get a new car, because we should all want to improve our life. What I am saying is that if you base how you feel and your inner security on the things that you have in life, you'll never find inner peace. Take the risk and stop comparing yourself to other people. I'm not even suggesting that you need to be grateful or anything like that either.

What I do believe is that life is like a tight rope and what we need to do is learn how to walk across our tight rope without falling off. Ever been to a circus and seen the people who walk a tight rope from one side all the way to the other end? If they make one small mistake, if they sway too much to one side then they fall off. Can you imagine being that high up in the air, walking on a wire with hundreds of people watching you? Yes these people are skilled professionals, and are highly trained. You know what else they do? They remain focused to help with their balance and every move they make is one step at a time. That's what we can learn from these people. If we sway too much to one side we're going to find ourselves constantly comparing ourselves to other people. If we sway too much to the other side we're always feel stuck in life and stuck in this cycle of self-doubt and pity. Either way we are bound to fall off our rope. Our task in life is to remain focused so we balance the things that we want and the things that we desire, while at the same time having self-reflection. If we can do this we'll not only be able to walk across our tight rope without falling off, but we'll be able to take risks in life as well.

Let's talk about gratefulness. I've never really liked it when people say "well you just need to be grateful." Well sometimes being grateful just doesn't fit. For example, two of my really good friends (Jeff and Joe), recently got two brand new trucks. Jeff got a brand new black on black Dodge Ram, while Joe got a new 2020 Ford F-350. Now just a little bit about me it has been my dream to own a brand new truck. I'm thinking I would look really good driving a black Ford Raptor with black rims and the windows tinted. In actuality, I drive a 2000 grey Honda Civic that has a mismatched colored driver rear view mirror. So when my two friends got their brand new trucks of course I felt a little jealous, but for anyone to suggest or tell me to just be grateful that I have a car is just plain foolish. OK so let me get this straight I'm supposed to feel grateful that I'm driving a car that has over 180,000 miles on it, while my two friends just got brand new trucks.

In this scenario I could have easily swayed to the left and started to compare where I'm at in life compared to my two friends. They have trucks and I'm driving a Honda Civic that most likely a donation center wouldn't accept. So if we can agree that comparing myself to my two friends isn't helpful, and being grateful just isn't realistic, what else could I do in this scenario? What else could I do to make sure I don't fall off my tight rope? How about just being happy for my two friends and celebrate their success with them. Yes it's natural for me to feel a little jealous of my two friends, but that doesn't mean I need to compare myself to them. In fact, what I could do is just be excited and truly happy for them and for their success.

If I'm able to change my mindset and not compare myself to them, but instead be proud of their success this will not only increase my own self-esteem, but also build theirs up as well. Gratefulness is an excellent quality to have, and on some level we all need to grateful for the things we have and the blessings in our life. However, you also can't force yourself to be grateful, just like you can't force yourself to be happy. Take someone who is miserable in their marriage and tell them to "just be grateful that they're married," and see what they tell you. If however, that person starts to work on their marriage and improve their connection with their spouse than yes they probably would feel grateful to be married. Gratitude comes from within. Start with the mindset that you're going not going to compare yourself to other people. It's a no win situation.

CHAPTER 3
LET THE POSITIVITY GROW

I USED TO have this supervisor who would constantly say "weed your garden." Shout out to Erin Ward. So let's talk about "weed your garden." Her perspective was that you constantly have to reevaluate your friendships and move on from those who do not support or accept you. One of the ways that you can control what you hear and control what you take in is to constantly weed your garden, and allow yourself to move on from people who are unsupportive of you. OK relax and take a deep breath. I know what a lot of you are thinking right now. How in the world do you just expect me to just ditch my friends? I completely understand that it probably seems more logical and makes more sense to keep your unsupportive friends rather than not having any friends at all. I get it, I really do. Making hard choices in life is never easy. In fact, even bringing up with the word change causes us to have anxiety and instantaneously shut down. Change is hard. Change is uncomfortable, but the good news is that we change every day whether we know or it. My guess is that by now you have either moved on from some of your peers, or you're in the reevaluation phase and are contemplating making some tough decisions.

Still, there are some of you who just can't hear this right now and think that it's nice having some friends to go out with regardless of how they act or how they treat you. Others of you may also be saying that your friends aren't really that bad and they just need to get to know you and once they do they'll start to accept you. So maybe you're right. People can change, and maybe it is better to have at least a few people in your corner rather than no one at all. But ask yourself this. How can you possibly feel good about yourself and find your voice if you are constantly surrounded by negativity?

If your goal in life is to finally start loving yourself, than start putting yourself first and start surrounding yourself with positive people. Positivity attracts positivity. Negativity brings us down, positivity builds us up. Wanna example? If you ever get the luxury of being in the position where you receive or obtain a lot of money (athletes, musicians, entrepreneurs, and especially lottery winners) the first thing people will tell you is to surround yourself with people who will support you as opposed to people who will just take advantage of you. Ever wonder how professional athletes who make millions of dollars are suddenly broke after they stop playing? It's because of the company they surrounded themselves with, and how these people only took advantage of them and their money. Now this might seem like a drastic example, but the principal and lesson here are the same. To me, the job of your support system is to build you up, not use you for their gain or take advantage of you either monetarily or for their amusement.

A really good and solid support system cares for you and helps you when you are at your worst, and doesn't give up on you when you're at your lowest. If right now you feel less than or unequal to society's standards based on your race, socioeconomic status, weight or appearance, one way to combat society's message of inequality is to surround yourself with people who can create and enforce a different inner belief in yourself. Want another example? Have you ever seen a movie where the cool kid in the group constantly uses another kid as the butt of his jokes or who only hangs out with this kid to make him feel better about himself? The entire audience can see that this other kid is getting used by the cool kid, but this other kid just can't see it for himself/herself. We've all been there including me. Trust me I know cutting people out of your life is a very hard thing to do. Some of you are wrestling with this right now. I can't promise you that everything will magically get better once you do this, because trust me life just doesn't work that way. It never does. What I can promise you is that if you don't do this than you'll never find inner happiness because you'll always be focused on trying to please other people.

Remember when I referenced how it took me over 30 years of my life to finally get to a place where I started to feel comfortable within my own skin? The main reason for this change was because I started to weed my own garden. Here's my disclaimer. Most of you who are reading this book know who you are. You know yourself and the areas you want to improve. You know your strengths, and you really know your weaknesses. However, if you are someone who is reading this book and constantly blame others for failed relationships both intimate relationships and also personal friendships you might want to look inwards and start asking yourself some very tough questions. Yes, it is not uncommon for friendships to change and at times even diminish. In fact, it is not uncommon for friendships to change during different stages of our life. For example, the friends you had in elementary school, most likely changed by the time you entered high school. However, if you are someone who ends friendships due to the sole purpose that the other person will not do what you say or act how you want them to act, than I'm sad to say that this says more about you than it does about them. As long as they are not breaking the law or doing something illegal if you try to manipulate or force your friends to conduct themselves in a certain way because you believe this is how they should act or this is how they should think, you will undoubtedly end up alone. Friendships are a two way street.

This section is designed for you to build up your support system, not re-enforce your inner belief that you are perfect and that other people need to serve your individual needs.

OK, so now that we got that out of the way, let's go back to controlling what you hear and also how to build up your support system. For this section I want to focus on two main areas that play very significant roles in our lives, family and work. Let's start with family.

Family

My guess is that growing up you heard this phrase from your parents at least one time in your life "yeah but they're family." No matter how much we sometimes wish that this wasn't the case, there is truth to the statement that "family is family." No matter how much we might want to, we can't just wish away our family, or wish we had different parents. Most importantly no matter how much we try, we most likely cannot change our family. They are who they are and most likely they are set in their ways. If this section doesn't imply to you than thank your lucky stars, but for many of us family have caused a significant amount of pain and hurt. Even worse families have also caused us to experience trauma and neglect. If this has happened to you, I'm truly sorry and I sincerely mean that. I have such a deep and profound level of respect and admiration for people who have gone through the worst of the worst, but yet keep doing the best that they possible can regardless of their upbringing. The people that fight tooth and nail for everything they have despite life never giving them a fair chance. You are my heroes, and you serve not only as an inspiration to me, but also for society as well.

Don't believe me? Who do you think people would rather

celebrate? An uplifting story of how someone triumphed and overcame all the obstacles and hurdles that life had to offer? Or the story of Richie Rich who inherited his parent's wealth and business, and who never had a single roadblock in his life growing up? Now I might be a little jealous of Richie Rich, but at the same time I could care less about his story. But, Richie made it in life. Who cares, he was supposed to make it, how could he not make it? Wealth, stability, inheritance, status. Richie was given every advantage that life could possibly hand him, as opposed to the person who had to overcome every obstacle and challenge that life could possibly offer. Broken family, no support, mental illness, yet somehow they manage to succeed in life. Now that's something to celebrate. The point here is to keep fighting, get help, and know that there are people rooting for you. There are people in your corner who want you to succeed and get better.

Now, let's get back to your family of origin and what to do if your family constantly shames you or puts you down. Sometimes it's neither plausible, nor realistic to just up and leave your situation and start over. Often, we have to make do with what we have. However, what we can do is put boundaries in place. In order to establish boundaries with your family, the first thing that I want you to do is put yourself first. That's right I said it, put what you want and what you need first. The hard part of setting boundaries is not only implementing them, but telling another family member "no" or "I'm not going to tolerate that behavior." Dr. Traci Lowenthal (2015), made the argument that by placing boundaries with family members you are not rejecting the actual person, but in fact you are rejecting their behavior. You're self-advocating for yourself thus growing as a person. You don't need to be mean or malicious, but I do want to encourage you to start standing up for how you want to be treated.

In her book, Michelle Weiner-Davis discussed a concept, "Acting as if." I talk about this concept a lot with parents. Say for example you want to talk to your kid about something important or something serious (sex, drugs, pornography). It's understandable that as a parent you might be a little nervous talking to your kid about any of the three above mentioned topics. If you go into the conversation timid and already have it in your head that this is not going to go well than most likely that is what will happen. If however, you go into the conversation acting confident in yourself even if you're not and believe that everything will be fine than that's how the conversation will go. It's the same thing with family. Imagine for a second that one family member that always gets under your skin. Do me a favor take a second and think about how you would not only like to act towards this family member, but also how you would like to feel as well. Now, take away the emotion and do this exercise again. A lot of you wish and dream about telling off certain family members from aunts and uncles, to in-laws, and even siblings as well. Some of them probably deserve it, but if you remove the emotion and rationally think about how you want to act and feel my thought is that a lot of you would come to the conclusion that really doing something like this is just not worth your time or energy. Whether they tease you, put you down, or simply disrespect you my guess is that you don't want what they do to upset or bother you. Essentially, you don't want what they do or say to have any effect on you, and you definitely don't want their actions to affect how you feel about yourself.

Christine Carter, came up with the phrase "Keep calm like a champion" (Carter, 2017). Ever watched a game or match that was so close, so intense that it caused you to have anxiety? Ever thought to yourself how professional athletes could remain so calm and collected under so much pressure? I know I have. I've watched sporting events that were so intense that I just couldn't remain seated. I had to get up and walk around because I was so nervous. To make it to that level, professional athletes have a different make up and a different gene that most of us don't have. What we can learn from professional athletes is the power and effectiveness of deep breathing. I promise you in order to get to that level athletes utilize and practice deep breathing and visualization on a regular basis. I'll go more in depth with deep breathing in chapter 5 so stay tuned, but next time you are at a family gathering or with your family during the holidays slow down your breathing and keep calm like a champion.

Work

For me to suggest to not allow work to affect you would not only be disingenuous, but it's just not reality. Work plays such a crucial role in our life from the moment we get our first job at 16, to when we actually start our careers and eventually retire. Meet anyone either on a first date or in a social gathering, and the first thing that people will ask you is "what do you do for work?" Work plays such a critical role in our lives, and often shapes our identities and values. Work as public servant (police, fire, EMT), you must be strong and brave. If you're an educator or a teacher you must be really caring and patient. If you're a doctor than you must be really smart. Work can either build us up and increase our inner confidence, or it can easily tear us down.

In the last Gallup poll that I read from September 2017, estimated that 85 percent of people worldwide hated their job. In the United States alone, 70 percent of people indicated that they hated their job. Not only did this Gallup poll suggest that 85 percent of people hate their job, but also indicated that the same number of people hated their boss as well. So let's agree that 85 percent of people is a really high number, and most likely that number is probably lower. A lot of factors could influence whether or not you like your job. For example, if someone took this poll, but was struggling in their marriage this would most likely affect how they feel about their job. The point here is that if right now you are struggling to get up every morning and go to work, I guarantee there are more people like you than there are people who love their job. Most of us just tolerate of our jobs simply because we have no other choice.

So what do you do if you really hate your job? What do you do if you're really miserable and just can't stand your boss? Most of us just can't quit on the spot and walk out of our job like you see in the movies. We have bills to pay, we have certain responsibilities, and quite honestly it's just not good practice to up and quit your job. Are there exceptions? Of course there are so before you tweet me yes there are exceptions to walking out on a job, i.e. sexual harassment, personal safety, and maybe even health reasons. There's nothing wrong with wanting better for yourself and wanting a job that you really enjoy. Isn't that what life is really about? I am not trying to advocate or tell you that you need to stay at your job especially if you are being subjected to a toxic or hostile work environment. If this is the case for you, than you'll need to ask yourself some very tough questions and come up with a plan. What I am trying to say is that no job is perfect. If you haven't realized it by now the perfect job just doesn't exist. There are pros and cons to every job, and there will always be other co-workers who you struggle to get along with.

Now back to work. If right now you're struggling with your job the general feedback you'll hear from other people is "just be grateful that you have a job right now." Remember the example I used earlier about gratefulness? The thing about gratitude is that yes it's an important value, but it's also a tricky concept as well. Right now, there are millions of people around this country who are out of work and are struggling to make ends meet.

There are parents who are struggling to put food on their table, and don't know how they are going to pay next month's rent/ mortgage. I'm even hesitant to talk about work, because of this issue. What I will say is that there is a fine difference between self-centeredness and modesty. Let me explain. Most of us struggle with some aspect of our job. Whether it's the pay, the work hours, the physical and mental demand, or coworkers/supervisors and upper management, there are several different things that affect us when it comes to work. However, we also fully understand that our life could look drastically different if we didn't have employment and want those who are out of work and who are struggling right now to find hope and success (modesty). In actuality, what we try to do is force ourselves to be grateful. We try and force ourselves to have the mindset to be grateful that I have a job when others don't. The problem here is that until your job is taken from you it's really hard to feel grateful when you just can't stand your job.

If right now you're struggling with gratitude, I don't think that this means you're selfish or self-centered. What that means is that you're human. Now, if you have the mindset that people who are unemployed are just lazy, and that you're better than them, well than that's a different story, and what you need to do is come down off your high horse and live in reality.

So what can you do if you right now you're really struggling to get up and go to work each morning? First, join the club. Statistics show that people call in sick on Mondays more than any other day of the week (Jio, 2009). Despite the struggles we all have with different aspects of our jobs, there are things that you can do to help yourself better appreciate and tolerate your job. Yes it's nice to get paid, but if you're like me all your money goes straight towards bills. It's actually pretty depressing to think about how all your hard earned money goes straight towards bills. So what else can you do to help yourself out especially on those Monday mornings? How about change your mindset.

If your company uses you for their labor and for their product, than why can't you use your job for your own benefit as well? Despite the job or the work environment could you make a goal of being more patient with other people? Could you use your job to try and improve your own self-confidence? Challenge yourself to do better. Use this time to prove to yourself that you are a strong person, and that whatever other people do or say will not affect how you feel about yourself or your job performance.

Former first lady, Michelle Obama, who exemplifies nothing short of class and professionalism, famously said in her 2015 democratic convention speech, "when they go low, we go high." What was once a really powerful idea has unfortunately turned into a catchphrase. There is however, a lot of truth to the statement, "when they go low, we go high." A couple of years ago I took this empowerment training that discussed the same concept of going high. The argument here is that by going high this increases our self-esteem and inner confidence, as opposed to going low which only bring us down.

So before the cynical side of you comes out just take a deep breath and really think about this for a second. We all have co-workers or supervisors who for whatever reason we just do not get along with. Just seeing them or even hearing their voice puts us in a bad mood. Now just imagine how satisfying this would be not only for you, but for everyone in your office/work building if you modeled what it looked like to take the high road. Challenge yourself to see the good in other people and push yourself to consistently take the high road. After that sit back and watch how this increases your self-esteem.

Build up your support system

So by now you're probably wondering how do I build up my support system, or how do I make better friends? If you did a search on the internet right now about how to build a support system, the most common theme you would read about is joining a support group. If you're depressed, then join a depression support group. Lost a family member or friend then join a grief group. Since losing my dad, my mother joined a widow's group that meets about once a month. There's a lot of truth and benefit of being around like-minded people who can relate and emphasize with what you're going through. Strength in numbers. The point here is to at the very least keep an open mind about support groups.

Facebook's new thing right now is promoting social groups. Anywhere from sports groups, to hiking groups, and food groups, and all the way to fashion groups as well. I'll address social media a little bit later in this section. If groups aren't for you I completely understand, but again would encourage you to just keep it in the back of your mind. The good news here is that there are other avenues as opposed to groups that you can explore as well.

First, let's figure out your passion and hobbies. If you like art, consider going to art events near your area. If your goal and desire is to get in better shape, then join a gym or fitness center. The thing about these two examples is that I promise you the more you go to social events or the more you go to the gym you will start seeing the same people over and over. I can't tell you how many new people I have met just by going to the gym on a regular basis. Next, decide for yourself who you would like to start getting to know and take the risk and introduce yourself. Say to the other person, "I'm so and so, and I see you here all the time." After that see where the conversation goes. Remember life is all about taking risk and trying new things. Get your ass out on the dance floor and start meeting new people. Plant different seeds and see what relationships start to blossom. I have learned that the more you put yourself out there and suggest different things to other people, the more this will be reciprocated. Watch how if you start to ask other co-workers out to lunch on a regular basis, that they too in return will include you the next they go out to lunch as well.

Look I'm not trying to suggest this will be easy, because it won't. In fact, most likely your offer might get rejected here and there. The thing here is that you have to start somewhere so why not now? Take the risk and start putting yourself out there. The more you do this the hope is that not only will you be included in lunch outings, but hopefully invited to happy hours after work, and movie outings on the weekend.

Back to social media. Full disclosure it took me a while to warm up to the idea of networking using social media platforms. My preference is that you build up your support system the old fashion way, face to face. I also understand and accept that if you use social media the right way it can also help increase your support system. However, there are things that I would like you to consider. 1). Yes, a lot of connection first gets started online. Clearly, it is much easier to connect online than it is in person. What I would argue is that we try and meet half-way on this. I concede that social media plays a huge role in our culture, and yes it might even be more important to have more friends online than actual real life peers. What I would like you to consider is trying to move at least some online friendships to more everyday real life interactions. Hence find a balance between online and real human connection. 2). Your mental health comes first. I'm not here to lecture you about social media and what you should or should not post, or how many times you should or should not be posting. Rather, I'm here to tell you that if you are using social media your mental health must come first. The hard truth about social media is that a lot us use it as a way to try and increase our self-worth. We base how many likes we get, and how many friends we have as a way to increase how we feel about ourselves. Of course, it feels good to have other people comment about the selfie we just posted and tell us how good we look. However, if you are using social media as a way to determine how you feel about yourself you are bound to be let down. Social media cannot be a measure of your inner self-worth. Control what you take in.

OK so now that we got that out of the way, let's get creative and think about other ways that we can build up your support system. How about using your pets and kids as a way to meet new people? That sounds bad right? But just hear me out. When my wife and I first got married we lived in a townhouse community. At that time we decided to get a dog which in return helped us to start meeting other dog owners within our complex. If right now you live in an apartment residence think about how many people you see on a regular basis, but have never really talk too. Just by having a dog, my wife and I met so many other couples. Some of the relationships/connections we made stayed on a surface level, but others evolved and grew to where we started to hang out and do social outings together. To this day, my wife and I still keep in touch with one other couple who lived right above us. Hello Ben and Emily. If getting a dog doesn't speak to you, volunteer at your church, join a book club, or start taking classes at your local rec center or library. Consider joining a bowling or softball league.

If you have kids right now you probably have either met or seen several different parents. Whether it's been through your kid's school, youth sports, or other community activities, you'll likely start to see and meet other parents through your child's interactions with other kids. Unlike adults, kids typically have an easier time making new friends. Kids have more time than adults, and on average kids can relate better to each other than adults can. Ever heard the saying that "kids are innocent?" Adults can learn a lot from kids. Unlike adults, kids aren't corrupted by the suspicion and fear of another person's race, background, or status. For the most part kids just want to play each other. Calm the part of you that is judgmental and disapproving. Start getting to know the other parents who you see on a regular basis. Set up play dates, get dinner together, but take the risk and put yourself out there.

Trust me, I know this is hard. For whatever reason, as parents we judge each other and try to present that everything is fine and that we're in control. When really we're not in control and are just doing the best that we can, and are figuring things out on the fly.

Will this work out every time for you? No it won't, but the more you put yourself out there the easier it gets. I know this is hard, or at least it was for me. I can still remember how nervous I was when I first asked these two other dads at my kid's daycare if they wanted to set up a play date and get our boys together over the weekend. That was over 4 years ago. Right now I couldn't imagine doing this parent thing without the help and support of the other parents (West, Marotz, and Fodens) who my wife and I met along the way. All it took was for me to put myself out there. The point here is that there are ways to build up your support system. All you have to do is get creative and start taking some risks. It's in you, now go out and do it.

CHAPTER 4
CONTROL WHAT ENTERS YOUR BODY

FOR THE MAJORITY of my adult life I have put my sole focus, energy, and time trying to improve and change my external appearance. To me the math was simple improve how I look, will help improve my self-confidence. So let's agree that improving your physical health is a very good thing. For good reason, our society focuses on health from what to eat, to anti-aging cream, and to the technology we buy which counts our calories and the amount of steps we take. However, I would argue that no matter how good or fit we look on the outside, only masks how we truly feel on the inside. Want an example? Ever seen the big, muscular guy at the gym that every guy thinks to themselves "man I wish I looked like that guy." Well bring in another guy that is bigger than guy number 1 and then guy number 1 all the sudden feels insecure about himself because he's no longer the biggest guy at the gym. Most people think why would guy number 1 feel insecure, he's like one of the biggest guys I have ever seen.

The dark truth about health and fitness is that we have to be careful to not let our obsession to be fit contribute to our insecurities. The premise here is that we have to change our system as a whole both externally and also internally as well. Things like yoga and meditation which focuses on improving our mental and emotional health are not only gaining in popularity, but are now being incorporated in schools and also in workplace trainings as well. I'll talk more about the mind/body connection in the next chapter. So again we can agree that getting healthier has many positive effects both physically, emotionally, and mentally as well. However, why don't we also try and agree that physical appearance alone by itself will not necessarily result in happiness. My argument here is that in order to improve your life and find happiness you will need to change a number of things in your life, not only just your physical appearance.

Want more proof? Look at me. Rewind back to my mid-twenties. No cardio for this guy, my sole focus was to get as big as possible. Eat, sleep, workout and get a bunch of tattoos. To me that was the key to feeling good about myself. Now in no way was I every guy number 1, but I do take pride in how I look. Ask anyone who knew me at that stage in my life and they will confirm that I thought the only way to feel good about myself and get noticed by the opposite sex was to look really good and be in the best shape of my life. It's not rocket science, if you're at a bar one of the ways to get noticed is to look really good. Now this felt good at the time, but what I slowly came to realize is that relationships would only go so far before there would be a mutual split. Once I got into a relationship my internal self would tell me to work out even harder to not only compensate how I felt inside, but also justify why this person was with someone like me. I couldn't really offer them any sort of emotional health/support because inside I felt weak and insecure. My rational was that this person was only with me because of the way I look, so therefore in order to keep the relationship I had to workout extra hard. So what do you think happened? That's right it was this vicious cycle that kept repeating itself?

Fast forward to today, I'm almost 40 years old and am now the guy at the gym who reeks of icy hot that nobody wants to be around. Health is especially important now that I'm getting older, but just like exercising my muscles I've also learned that I have to exercise and improve my emotional health as well.

The hardest lesson that I think we all have to learn in life is that we can blame whatever circumstance we want, and trust me there are some very real and valid situations, but we also need to decide where we go from here and what we want to do with our life moving forward. Last chapter I went over trying to control what we hear, now let's go over what enters our body.

One change that I think we can make right now is making more of a conscious effort of what we eat and what we consume. I recently met with a new client whose main complaint was severe anxiety and depression. After going over his history, we then addressed his diet. This client described his morning routine as drinking anywhere from three to four cups of coffee for breakfast and then having fast food along with a coke for his lunch break. OK, so clearly I needed to do a lot of work around changing what enters his body from the amount of caffeine he intakes, to reducing the amount of sugar he consumes, and getting him to make healthier food selections. However, if right now you are feeling some judgement towards this guy or anyone else who struggles with their diet, I would remind you that we are a society based on doing what's easier and what takes less effort. High speed internet isn't enough anymore we now need 3x high speed internet.

Simply put it is easier to eat fast food than putting the effort into cooking healthier. I never thought in a million years that I would be the parent who takes their kids to McDonalds, but guess what I do when my wife's out of town. It's just easier and makes our life simpler to eat fast food rather than to cook healthy. However, go back to chapter 3, Let the Positivity Grow. If you know someone who is depressed or anxious, encourage them to start eating healthy. If you're depressed, cooking for yourself takes every single ounce of energy you possess. Every part of you says "just pick something up on your way home." The mere thought of going to the grocery store and then having to be around other people causes so much stress and panic that severely depressed people just give up and shut down. If you know someone like this, team up with them and start making healthier choices together.

The Case against Alcohol and Marijuana

Most of you reading this book are probably in your early to middle adulthood. If by this time you have figured out that you need to make life changes and getting rid of alcohol is one of them than good for you. If you're reading this book and have a significant history of alcohol and/or substance abuse- get help. For every alcohol advertisement promoting the glamorous lifestyle of hanging out on a beach drinking with friends, there's also ads that endorse legitimate treatment facilities that help promote and treat alcohol and substance abuse. Call these facilities, talk to an intake counselor, and get the help you deserve.

For most of us reading this book alcohol has plays a huge role in our lives, and even worse the alcohol industry knows it. From advertisements, to sponsorships and endorsements, and to celebrity branding the alcohol industry is a multi-billion dollar industry that's only getting bigger. Ever notice that every commercial for alcohol contains the hottest people you can possible find? Nowadays you can't even go to the grocery store, or go to a coffee shop without alcohol being thrown in your face. However, let's do an experiment and write down a list of the most regrettable, disappointing, and shameful moments of your life. Now look at the list and determine what's the single most common factor that connects all of those events? That's right alcohol.

Now I am not trying to justify anyone's behavior or choices, or suggest in any fashion that alcohol should be used as an excuse for your poor decisions. What I am suggesting is that for a lot of us alcohol has done nothing but disconnected our families, caused us legal issues, and subjected us to abuse and neglect. The truth here is that you cannot start feeling better about yourself, while at the same time constantly drink alcohol. The two just do not go hand in hand. So let's do an experiment over the next month and significantly reduce the amount of alcohol you consume and see how this improves your mood, your health, and see how it also improves your personal and intimate relationships. Will it be hard yes- our society promotes alcohol. Are you going to the game, better have a beer while doing it, or better yet meet up before the game and pound as many beers as you possible can before you enter the stadium. This way you not only do you save money, but get a good buzz before you have to pay twice the amount for a drink.

Some of you right now are reading this saying to yourself that I drink socially and there's nothing wrong with that or with me. I drink with friends at social gatherings and not you or anyone else can convince me otherwise. OK I can hear that, and a large part of me understands that as well. After a hard work week, there's nothing more satisfying than being around good company and enjoying a drink together. I'm not here to tell you what to do. In fact, some of my closest friends who are reading this right now i.e.- Jeffrey, JW, and Joe are planning the next "Dad's night out." If your reply back to me right now is "screw you I'm fine," then think about this for a second. What does it say about you that you have to drink? Well it says that I like to drink socially. It says that I like to have fun. OK, so again I get it. We only live once right? Slow down right now and really think about this. When we categorize any behavior i.e. social drinker as opposed to an alcoholic, what are we really doing? We're justifying and rationalizing our behavior. If we tell ourselves "I drink because I have a stressful job." OK, now remove the rationale as to why you drink alcohol and what are you left with? The truth is we try and justify why we drink (stress, need to relax), and if that doesn't work we give ourselves a more socially acceptable label (moderate drinker), as opposed to a more severe label (alcoholic).

The point here is that again if your goal right now is to start feeling better about yourself, than again I'm sorry to say drinking alcohol won't help you get to that goal. Before I lose you completely just stay with me for a moment and let's go over the facts about alcohol. After that it's all up to you.

Facts about Alcohol

Fact number 1, alcohol is a depressant. What does this mean? A lot of people drink alcohol to feel better. Had a really bad week or a fight with your spouse? What do most people do? Have a drink or in a lot of cases have a few. However, have you ever noticed what happens to your mood after you drink alcohol on a regular basis? Most people are aware of how their body feels. We feel sluggish, we might have a headache, our stomach hurts, and we feel tired. Nevertheless, just like our bodies, alcohol also affects our emotions. In her article published in the American Addiction Centers, Meredith Watkins, MFT (2020), that "while alcohol may temporarily relieve some of the symptoms of depression, it ultimately serves to worsen depression on a long-term basis" (Watkins, 2020). The hard truth here is that alcohol is not only a depressant, but also a sedative as well. If you consistently drink to numb your problems, well one or two things are going to happen. A). You're going to keep drinking- which is not good right? Or B). When you wake up the next day, your problems will still be there and either you have to deal with them, or go back to A. For the third time, I'm sorry to say but you cannot start feeling better about your life if you are constantly drinking alcohol.

Fact number 2, alcohol slows down brain function thus alters brain chemistry. Alcohol slows down neurotransmitters that communicate or send signals from the brain to the rest of your body (Alcohol Addiction Center, 2019). More specifically alcohol affects two types of neurotransmitters- excitatory and inhibitory neurotransmitters. Alcohol suppresses the release of glutamate (excitatory neurotransmitter) and increases another neurotransmitter GABA (inhibitory) (DiSalvo, 2012). So what does this mean? When you are intoxicated your balance, vision, thought process, and behavior become impaired. OK, so this makes sense right? You drink high amounts of alcohol, and then as a result you get drunk. What I want you to consider is this. If alcohol affects normal brain chemistry by suppressing and increasing certain neurotransmitters to the point where brain function and brain activity slow down, do you think you would have gotten in that bar fight, or made that poor decision if you were sober? Of course you wouldn't. So is it worth it? Is it really worth getting so intoxicated to the point where your thought process becomes so altered to the point where you struggle to control your own behavior?

Fact number 3, alcohol increases the release of dopamine. The thing about drinking alcohol is that if you're really stressed or upset alcohol makes you feel relaxed right? If you're sad, it makes you feel better in the moment. Why? Because, "alcohol increases the release of dopamine in your brain's reward center" (DiSalvo, 2012). One of the reasons why many people struggle with just drinking one or two alcoholic drinks is because of the release of dopamine. So what's the problem? Go back to fact number 1. Alcohol is a depressant. Alcohol tricks your mood. It tells you to keep drinking to feel better, but what it really does is affect your mood and is also harmful to your health.

Fact number 4, drinking high levels of alcohol on a regular basis shrinks your brain. Hear me out and let me put this fact in context. As we age, it's only natural for our brain function and brain volume to change. Take for example dementia which is typically not diagnosed until the later stages of life. Why? Mostly notably, Alzheimer's disease affects different areas of the brain including damages to the frontal and temporal areas of the brain (Landon-Romera, Kumfor, Irish, & Piguet, 2016). This prohibits neurons and brain cells the ability to communicate with each other. In addition, as the disease (Alzheimer's, Dementia) progresses different areas of the brain begin to shrink (Landon-Romera et al., 2016). I am not trying to suggest or indicate by any means that if you drink alcohol you will automatically get dementia later in life. What I am trying to do is present scientific based evidence about what alcohol does to your system and to your brain. Drinking high amounts of alcohol will over time decrease brain mass. If right now you are struggling with alcohol abuse/dependence I would really encourage you to do more research about the correlation of alcohol and dementia. None of us are invincible. Whatever we put in our bodies on a long term basis including alcohol will catch up to us.

The last fact I want to discuss is more for parents who are reading this book. Fact number 5, more adolescents use alcohol than cigarettes or marijuana (National Institute of Alcohol Abuse and Alcoholism, 2017). Researchers and scientist vary as to what age the brain fully develops, but the general census seems to be around age 25. In fact, adolescence is viewed as a critical time for brain development. If a human brain does not fully develop until the age of 25, and if you introduce a chemical or substance to that structure than this will undoubtedly change and alter brain chemistry. Susan Tapert, of the University of California, San Diego studied two different groups of adolescents. One group binged drank and the other group did not. Studies indicated the group that binged drank showed damage nerve cells, decline in white matter, and abnormal functioning in the hippocampus (Trudeau, 2015).

Change is never easy, especially reducing or eliminating

something that we enjoy and that our culture promotes. Make a list of the positives and negatives of reducing the amount of alcohol you drink, and I promise you the list of positives will significantly outweigh the list of negatives.

Marijuana

Before we even get started, yes I know you're already telling yourself, "there's nothing I could possibly say that will change your mind about marijuana." I know what you're already going to say, "it relaxes me," or "it calms me down," or "it helps me sleep." I get it. Marijuana is now mainstream, and by my count there are now 11 states that have legalized marijuana with probably more on the way.

When I was growing up, the country of Denmark was the talk of my peer group and how it was legal in that country to smoke marijuana out in the open. Fast forward 25 years later, there's now a marijuana shop on every street corner in my home state of Colorado. Marijuana is everywhere and the industry is only getting bigger. From CBD, to edibles, to good old fashioned weed and to now vaping, marijuana is an emerging industry. Since I was a kid there has always been this ongoing debate about marijuana. If you're for it, it's good for you; if you're against it, then it's bad for you. If don't care either way, you just hope your kid doesn't do it. The thing about this debate is that if I told you to do research on marijuana, what you'll do in return is find articles that support your position.

Really we do this with any debate or with any position we have. We find articles, facts, and other people that reinforce our position, then go to our corner and accuse the other side of not listening. Are there exceptions and cases where marijuana helps with certain medical conditions? Yes absolutely, i.e., Tourette's syndrome, chronic pain, and cancer to name a few.

What I want you to consider is this.

Number 1, there are other ways other than marijuana that can help you reduce stress. For example, deep breathing, mindfulness, meditation, and yoga are all things you can do other than marijuana. What you're going to tell me is that "I've tried deep breathing and it doesn't really work for me and the only thing that helps calm me down is marijuana." OK, I can hear that. You're also going to tell me, "that weed is natural and that it comes from the earth so therefore it's not bad for me." Well there are a lot of things that are "natural" but that doesn't necessarily mean that they're good for you. There are certain plants that are toxic and if eat them it could lead to potential death. If you're pregnant doctors warn against eating raw fish due to the risk of mercury and what that could do to your baby. So let's be honest. What you're really trying to tell me is that you just like to smoke weed.

Number 2, are the risk really worth the reward? Things that you are probably aware of, but are willing to overlook is that marijuana affects your cognition, and your physical and reproductive health. What you might not know is that marijuana has also been linked to gum disease and testicular cancer (Davis, 2020). The tricky part here is that to the exact extent marijuana affects your mental and physical health is an ongoing debate. So is it worth it? Is it worth exposing yourself to the possibility of developing a mental illness just to get high? Go back to deep breathing and meditation for a second. The thing here is that you will not find any credible article on the harmful effects of deep breathing and the potential risk it causes to your mind and body. The same can't be said about marijuana.

Number 3, the gateway to other drugs debate. Full disclosure, I'm not a substance counselor nor do I want to be. I don't advertise or promote myself as being an expert on substance abuse, and would need to refer out if a client came into my office wanting substance abuse treatment. However, when it comes to the debate as to whether or not marijuana is a gateway drug to other substances I am on the side that marijuana is absolutely a gateway drug. Ask any recovering addict, or someone who has experimented with different drugs, what their first drug was and they will you it was marijuana. Does this mean that everyone who smokes marijuana will automatically use other drugs? No of course not. At the same time statistics indicate that there is more of a likelihood you will experiment with other drugs if you use marijuana on a regular basis. Think about it for a second. If the opportunity presents itself, who do you think is more likely to use a different drug other than marijuana? Somebody who already uses marijuana, or somebody who has never tried marijuana ever in their life? Despite the what society says it is possible to live a life without marijuana. Again, I am not a substance abuse therapist, but I do work with families, and have parents come in my office all the time due to their child smoking marijuana.

I always tell parents that yes weed is part of our culture, but now is the time to get ahead of this. From movies, to music, to athletes and entertainers, marijuana is everywhere we look. However, my number one issue with marijuana is that yes I believe it is a gateway to other drugs. If right now you're a parent start planting seeds (no pun intended) to your child that they don't need to use marijuana, that they're better than that. Start planting seeds that marijuana won't help them achieve their goals, or get them to where they want to be in life. Start planting these seeds, and the next time your child is presented with smoking weed with his/her friends, these seeds will start to grow and they'll soon realize that they are better than that, and that marijuana isn't going to help them in life. If right now you're smoking marijuana on a regular basis try using other relaxation skills to help calm and soothe you. Before the cynical and skeptical part of you comes out give deep breathing, meditation, and yoga a chance. Allow yourself to do something different and start practicing these skills on a regular basis. Take the risk, improve your life, and move on from marijuana.

CHAPTER 5
COGNITION

IF RESEARCH SHOWS that we can become our worst critics, then why can't we also be our best cheerleaders as well? What would happen if we started to change our language and started using more positive and uplifting language to describe our efforts, abilities, and our characteristics?

I started to really notice this with my kids and how their language would reflect their internal belief in themselves. When asked to spell a word or try something new my kids, especially my oldest would respond by saying "I can't do it." My wife and I are now making a conscience effort to try and catch this now, and work with them on changing their mindset before it's too late. So when they say things like "I can't," we correct them and instead have them say things like "I'll get it," or "I'm trying my best." So what would happen if we did the same thing as adults?

If you're thinking to yourself "well I'm not a kid this sounds stupid," then you're right at least about the first part. You're not a kid and as such this is going to be one of the most difficult things to do. In fact, the negative language we use as adults only intensifies and gets worse as we age. For example, ever told yourself "I'm worthless," or "I'm unlovable," or even worse "I'm stupid?" As adults everything we do is set in place by now. From what we like and not like, to our daily routine, even to the way we fight and argue. We're creatures of habit. Help me out married couples. When you and your spouse get into an argument, ever notice that you want your partner to act a certain way, but always find that they always go back to their old habits. Why? Because, our brains are wired to always go back to what we know.

In her book, "Divorce Busting," Michelle Weiner-Davis, talked about an experiment with mice and how mice were placed in a maze and at the end of the maze were rewarded with cheese. Mice would go down the same tunnel each time, and each time it would be the same end result- cheese. However, when the cheese was removed, mice would stop going down that initial tunnel and instead would adjust and go down other tunnels looking for cheese (Weiner-Davis, 2008). Ms. Weiner-Davis argues that as adults we keep doing the same thing over and over again expecting there to be cheese at the end of the tunnel even if there's not. Why? Because, again we are creatures of habit.

Unlike adults, kids can have an easier time adjusting and adapting. However, if you're like me negative self-talk has become second nature. Our challenge is to start working on controlling and managing our thought process. For example, there are some people right now thinking to themselves, "Justin wrote a book, well it's probably not any good." Now my immediate thought is well those people can go fuck themselves. If however, I slow myself down and change my thought process I instead can chose to not focus on what other people think, but instead be proud that I did something that I have wanted to do for the past several years. Conversely, if my cognition stayed on the initial thought of "Justin's book is stupid," than my mind would naturally travel back to failures and mistakes all the way dating back from high school and beyond.

Our challenge in life is to start controlling what enters our body from the food we eat, to the thoughts we have, and to the words we hear. Now some of this we can control, and some it we're just going to have to do the best we can. What we can control is the way we talk about ourselves, and start using more positive language. See chart 2, Changing Language. Before we talk about self-soothing skills, let's first go over taking out your trash and also the role of the brain, and parts of the brain that affect and control our cognition.

Chart 2

Negative self-talk	*Positive self-talk
- I'm not worth it	- I'm trying by best
- There's no use	- I never give up
- I can't do it	- I enjoy life to the fullest
- I'm a failure	- I endeavor to the best I can be
- I'm stupid	- I value my work
- I always mess things up	- I am a valued employee
- People don't like me	- I radiate love and others reflect love back to me
- I'm ugly	- I am enough
- I'm a bad person	- I see others as good people who are trying their best
- I'm unlovable	- I am lovable and a loving person
- I'm fat	- I accept the shape of my body and I find it beautiful and appealing
- I'm a mean person	- I accept others for who they are

*Retrieved from Mindvalley, January 2019

Take out the Trash

Growing up part of my weekly chore list included what my parent's called a "trash run." Every week I went from room to room throughout my house emptying out all the house trash into a large plastic bag. As a kid I got into this routine where I would start the trash run upstairs by first emptying out the trash from each bedroom, and then make my way towards the main floor kitchen trash, and then end downstairs where our laundry room was located. I would of course also make sure to empty out all the bathroom trash as well. From there I was expected to take out all the trash and put it at the end of our driveway for the garbage man to come and pick it up.

We all do this right? It's pretty simple when our kitchen trash is overflowing we empty it and either run it out to the trash can in the garage, or you take it out to your community dumpster. However, when I was a teenager instead of emptying out each trash can like I was supposed to, I would instead push the trash down to make more room in the trash can and then wait until the following week to empty out the trash. This is the same process of what we do with negative thoughts. Starting when we are teenagers we get in the habit of just pushing negativity down to the point where it gets stuck and embedded inside of us.

For many of us, adolescence was this challenging time in life where we tried to establish our independence, figure out who we are and who we want to be, while at the same time trying to process and adjust to physical and social changes. Adolescence is typically the stage where teenagers start to experiment with drugs and alcohol, get bullied for the first time, and have their first encounter with the justice system as well. Moreover, this is also the stage in life where teenagers start to experience and feel very complicated and difficult emotions from depression and anxiety, to heartache and confusion over their first real break-up. Adolescence is not only hard for the teenager, but equally challenging for the parent(s) as well.

Nonetheless, adolescence is also the stage in life where we are the most impressionable. Teenagers take in everything, and are influenced both positively and negatively as well i.e. peer pressure.

This is also the stage in life where we start to develop an inner belief in ourselves. What teenagers are told and what they hear, how they're treated, and how they're viewed by other people play a vital role in how they will feel about themselves. From coaches, to teachers and administrators, to peers, and most importantly to parents this is the stage of life where we start to develop an inner belief in ourselves.

If you're athletic than most likely you're considered popular; if you're the defiant kid you're most likely considered cool. If you're really smart than you might be considered odd, and if you're into drugs and goth well than most likely you're viewed as being rebellious. If you don't fit into the four above mentioned categories than most likely you're just doing the best that you can to survive. The point here is that for many of us, adolescence was the beginning point where we started to stuff and internalize every negative belief, every negative perception, and every negative word. If you think this is bullshit, and adolescence really wasn't that bad well than maybe it wasn't for you, but I would also have you consider this. If adolescence isn't really all that bad than why does teenage suicide keep increasing every year? In 2017, suicide was the second leading cause of death between the age group of 15 to 24 (Santhanam, 2019). This rate increased from 6.8 percent from 2000 to 2007, to 10.6 percent in 2017 (Santhanam, 2019).

What I'm telling you right now isn't designed to scare you, but we can't continue to fool ourselves that this isn't happening and this isn't real. Teens nowadays are subjected to online bullying and social media bullshit that thank goodness wasn't around when I was growing up.

If you're a parent right now the time is now to start emptying out your child's trash can. Don't wait till your kid's trash can gets over flowed and you have no choice but to empty it. Start the process now, and realize that this is a critical period where you can make the most impression in your child's life. Fill them confidence and inner security. Despite what other people think, teenagers are very self-aware and can hear and feel everything. If you don't want your kid to grow up being anxious and insecure in themselves start the process now and help them empty out their trash. Replace all the despair, negativity, and apprehension with hope, strength, and unconditional love.

Help your kid learn relaxation techniques that will help regulate their emotions, and calm their cognition. I'll go over deep breathing exercises with you later in this chapter. The same goes to the rest of you as well. Let this be the time that you finally empty out your trash can. Let this be the time that you finally do away with all the self-doubt and insecurity that has consumed you for years. Empty out all of your failures and regrets that put them in a large trash bag for the garbage man to pick up. Allow yourself to press reset and fill your body with a renewed sense of purpose. Ever been told that "you're not good enough," or that "you're a failure," or that "you're fat and ugly?" Now is the time to take out your trash.

The Human Brain

From the words we speak, to how we process information, and to how we move our body, the human brain is the central organ in everything we do. In fact, a focal point in psychotherapy is trying to help clients change their cognition. From EMDR, to CBT, and to DBT these types of therapy modalities focus on changing maladaptive and negative thought content. One of the harder challenges we face is to allow ourselves to move on from very painful and hurtful experiences that affect how we think and feel. In order to accomplish this difficult task we first need to understand the human brain.

First, there are an estimated 100 billion neurons in the human brain that continually receive information from each other (Amthor,

2012). Neurons send electrical signals to each other and receive information in two different ways. Dendrites receive incoming information, while axons send signals away from the cell to other neurons (Carter, 2010). Now imagine for a moment that a dendrite and neuron are about to communicate with each other. In order to this, the dendrite and neuron meet at what's described as a tiny gap called the synapse. Along with being "the most fundamental computing element in the nervous system" (Amthor, 2012), the synapse allows axons to release neurotransmitters thus permitting signals to be passed from one neuron to another neuron (Carter, 2010). In addition, I also want to note that there are three main parts of the synapse.

OK, so I know that was a lot to take in. Let's do this. Do me a favor and raise your left arm high in the air and wiggle your fingers as fast as you can. Pretty simple task right? In actuality, doing something like this that we do on an everyday basis takes hundreds of neurons inside our brain firing together and traveling together and then sending impulses down to our muscles. The point here is that everything we do starts with our brain.

Second, the brain is divided into two hemispheres- the right and left hemisphere. Split the brain right down the middle and hence you have a right and left hemisphere. Roger S. Sperry originated the theory of the "right and left brain theory," indicating that speech as well as critical and analytical thinking are controlled by the left side of our brain, while the right side tends to be more expressive and creative (Cherry, 2020). Since this theory emerged, other people have expanded on this and came up with concepts of their own. I'll let you do your own research as to the validity of the right brain/left brain theory. The point here is that these two hemispheres communicate with each other through the corpus callosum (Cherry, 2019).

Third, there are four main parts of the brain. This includes the cerebral cortex, cerebellum, limbic system, and the brain stem. Let's stay with the limbic system for a moment. The limbic system consists of the amygdala, thalamus, hypothalamus, and hippocampus (Amthor, 2012). If we go a little further and break down these brain structures we can then talk about their relevance in a negative thought cycle.

Let's start with the hippocampus. Ever wonder why we remember certain things and why certain things seem to be embedded in our memory? The hippocampus plays a vital part in our ability to move memories from short term to long term memories (Amthor, 2012). In addition, the hippocampus also plays "a critical role in the formation, organization, and storage of new memories as well as connecting certain sensations and emotions to these memories" (Cherry, 2019). Think about your life for a second. There are some things that you have either learned or experienced that are readily available whether you want them to be or not. Then there are the other things that you have learned or experienced that you either just ignore or forget. The learning and storage of memory is largely based on repetition. The more you do something the more it becomes second nature. Hence "practice makes perfect." This type of learning is described as disposable learning (Amthor, 2012).

Other types of learning are based on pleasure and the absence of negative emotions. This brings us to the Amygdala. Described as an almond shape mass of nuclei, the amygdala plays a significant role in emotional responses, hormonal secretions, and also memory (Bailey, 2018). If you take a test and see this question, "what part of the brain is known for fight, flight, or freeze?" The answer is the amygdala. Ultimately, emotion plays a crucial role in learning and memory. If something you do results in pleasure, than most likely you'll keep doing that exact same thing. If however, the end result is not pleasurable, and instead causes a negative feeling or emotion, than the likelihood of that behavior decreases. Nobody wants to feel bad about themselves, so if you do something and if that end result causes feelings of shame or guilt, than most people won't repeat that same behavior. Why is this important? Rita Carter argues that because "the amygdala is responsible for generating negative emotions, so to prevent them flooding the brain this part of the limbic system must be quiet" (Carter, 2010, p. 103). Part of the brain's function is based on survival. It tells us to eat to survive and run when there's danger. However, in order for us to avoid a heightened state of anxiety, we must be able to calm ourselves internally. This requires us to use different parts of our brain, while at the same time calming our limbic system.

Negative Thought Cycle

We are creatures of habit. So, if we get triggered (which causes us to cycle in a negative thought pattern), our system will focus on painful and hurtful events that have been encoded in our brains. I describe this as "the snowball effect". Imagine you are a little kid again, and after a big snowstorm you go outside to build a snowman. You put on your winter coat, hat and gloves, and you start building the base of your snowman. You start by packing snow together into a ball, and then start rolling that ball of snow throughout your front lawn. What started as just a small ball of snow has now become a massive snowball. This is the same thing that happens when we get stuck in a negative thought cycle. What starts off small (the triggering event), can quickly turn into a cycle of self-blame, shame, and doubt.

So, what do you do if you are stuck in a negative thought cycle? The first thing is to try and recognize what is happening so that you can allow yourself to do something different. Imagine a cycle that starts at point A (trigger), and then goes back to prior mistakes or a painful event (point B), followed by thinking about another event that caused guilt, shame, or regret (point C). After point C, your mind then travels to embarrassing or sad incidents that cause you to feel distress and self-doubt. Think back to when you had a fight with your spouse, or best friend. We replay that event over and over in our mind, and as we're doing this we get "flooded" with more and more emotion. At this point we're so flooded that we don't think rationally, and every type of negative thought content enters our head. Why does this happen?

Meet the subgenual prefrontal cortex (PFC). This area of the brain is part of the prefrontal cortex and is described as the emotional control center (Carter, 2010). The PFC is also the region of the brain that is most active during rumination and daydreaming. When the PFC is active, it's hard for us to rationally self-reflect, which causes our brains to engage in repetitive negative thinking (Greenberg, 2017). Let's now focus on a few self-soothing skills.

Deep Breathing

Along with identifying and recognizing that you're in a negative thought cycle, it will be very important moving forward that we identify some tools that you can use to help calm yourself internally, and stabilize those areas of the brain that were previously discussed. Let's start with deep breathing. Even as a therapist it took me awhile to really understand and grasp the importance of deep breathing. It's not that I didn't understand the value of deep breathing, but it really took me having kids and doing an EMDR training to really understand the significance of deep breathing. Call me a late bloomer, but my therapy practice now centers around deep breathing. In fact, deep breathing is also being incorporated in schools and also work place trainings as well. Consider for a second the last time you felt either scared or upset. Ever notice what happens to your system?

Whenever we are scared or upset our systems naturally shoot up and we stop breathing. Remember the amygdala which was previously discussed and how it controls the flight, fight, or flee response. Go back to my two boys for a second. If they are really upset or scared or feeling any sort of complicated emotion I know as a parent that their systems have shut down and that they have stopped breathing. What I have to do as their parent is regulate my system by intentionally controlling and monitoring my breathing cycle to help calm them down. In order to function our system has to be working and for that to happen your breathing has to be stable and consistent. Imagine your emotions on a scale of 1 to 10. If you're anywhere close to 10 than your system has already shut down and you're cognition is likely thinking about anything and everything. At that point what we have do is get you down to a 2 or a 1, so can start thinking rationally. If you already think that this is stupid, consider for a second the example I used of the professional athlete in chapter 3. I promise you superior athletes and professional entertainers practice deep breathing on a consistent basis to calm their internal systems so that they can perform on such a high level. Ever seen a baseball player step out of batter box for a moment, or a basketball player about to shoot a free throw? Ever notice how they take deep breaths to calm their nerves and refocus themselves?

So let's go over how to practice deep breathing, and let's start by doing a couple of things. First, with your eyes open or closed (I always close my eyes) try to pinpoint the areas of your body that either feel tense or heavy. What I want you to start doing is really try and start to know yourself internally. Notice the next time you feel upset or anxious and your body's internal response. For me, if my stomach feels tight or in knots, and if my legs feel heavy I know it's time for me to collect myself and spend a moment deep breathing. Next, start to deep breath. Breath in, hold it for a second and then exhale. Feel your breath as it enters your body and as it leaves as well. Thirdly, don't try to force anything. If a thought comes in your mind or if start to replay an event just let it happen, but simply go back and focus on your breaths. Allow your entire focus and energy be centered on the breath coming into your body and your breath exiting as well. I promise you if you stay with deep breathing you will not only feel more centered and balanced, but you will also feel the parts of your body start to drop and relax as well. Continue deep breathing until you feel you internal system return to baseline.

Calm Place

I was first introduced to calm /safe place during an EMDR training this past spring 2019. Essentially, calm place is a relaxation technique commonly used in EMDR therapy. Think of safe place as an emotional sanctuary where you can go to feel emotionally stable (Larsen, 2016). In EMDR therapy, safe place is part of the preparation phase and is one of the steps in 8 step therapeutic model. For the purpose of this section I am only going to discuss the first 2 steps of safe place.

The first step that I want you to do is bring up a place or an image that brings you to a place where you feel calm and at peace. As Francine Shapiro noted "for those clients who are unable to feel safe because of the nature of their trauma (e.g., sexual abuse or combat), it is best to identify and focus on a place that allows them to feel calm (Shapiro, 2018 p. 246). When I did this exercise I instantaneously imagined standing on the beach in Mexico. For me the beach is a place that immediately brings me a sense of relaxation and tranquility. When I do this exercise with my clients, some have imagined being in the mountains, while others have envisioned vacation cabins and mountain lakes. Whatever the scenario, make safe place something that is uniquely yours, and that you can go to whenever you're feeling any sort of challenging or troubling emotions.

The next step is to focus on the image and allow your body to feel all the emotions associated with the image while at the same time locating where in your body you feel the physical sensations (Shapiro, 2018). My encouragement to you is to really allow yourself to enter your safe place and imagine what you're feeling and also use all of your senses. If I were to go to my safe place (the beach in Mexico), and really take myself there, I can envision standing at the beach and feeling the sand underneath my feet. I can see the Pacific Ocean for miles, I can hear the birds chirping, and the waves crashing into the shoreline. I can feel the warmth on my skin, and smell the ocean breeze. My encouragement to you is to not only go deep into you safe place and use your senses, but also allow yourself to stay in your safe place until you feel emotionally balanced.

CHAPTER 6
FROZEN

WHETHER WE KNOW it or not, we learn something new every day. From childhood, to the day we die we are constantly taking in new information. Typically kids move through stages of development where they learn and develop different physical traits, social norms, and intellectual capabilities. Not every kid is the same and kids grow and mature at different rates, but on average kids are always learning. There are of course exceptions, i.e. learning disabilities, but as adults we can learn a lot from our kids. For example, unlike kids, adults pick and choose what new information we want to let in, and what we're receptive too. Kids really have no choice they have to learn what's in front of them or they don't receive a passing grade. However, the thing about kids is that they're unbiased; they're more curious, and less judgmental than adults. As adults we chose what we want to learn, what we want to hear, what we want to read, and what we want to watch. Even worse we have the perspective that if you're not on my side than you're against me. What I'm going to ask you to do is challenge yourself to learn something new today and be open-minded to the movie "Frozen." In particular, I'm going to ask you to be open-minded to the message that "Frozen," portrays to its audience.

Before we get started let me first acknowledge that yes "Frozen," is a kid's animated movie that is rated G, and that yes, I know that I'm comparing real life to a child's movie. In addition, I completely understand that real life rarely if ever has a Hollywood ending. If you haven't figured it out by now, my life is anything but a fairy tale. Just stay with me and keep an open-mind to the fact that everyone regardless of their age learns something new every day. This can even include how adults can learn how to change their life by simply listening to the message of a child's movie like "Frozen."

Growing up there was a period where my two boys just loved the movie "Frozen." Now I'm pretty sure you've probably seen this movie, but for me I can't tell you how many times I must have seen this movie. There was a time in my house, where this movie played at least three times a week for a span of about four months straight. Now since then my boys have outgrown "Frozen," and have moved on to Avengers and Power Rangers, but for span of time it was Frozen all day, every day. When we would run errands my oldest would bring his stuffed Olaf with him, and at night my wife and I would have to read "Frozen" bed time stories. We even went to "Frozen on Ice," as a family.

If you haven't seen the movie let me explain. The basic theme of the movie is to let go of your anger, embrace who you are, and start trusting people again. Elsa (one of the main characters), was born with the magical ability to create ice either through the use of touch or by using her enchanted powers. After her parents died, Elsa became Queen of Arendale, but after objecting to her sister Anna's engagement, Elsa's powers were then revealed. This is where the plot thickens. After Elsa's powers were discovered, Elsa then runs to the mountains to not only protect herself, but also protect everyone else from her powers. Elsa was made to feel ashamed of who she really is, but after learning how to control her powers she ends up embracing who she is, and in the process was also able to start loving other people as well. So of course this is the short version of the movie and there are other plots and twist and turns throughout the movie including the plot of the bad character (Hans). What I want to discuss further with you are the major themes of "Frozen" including letting go of anger, embracing who you are, and trusting other people again.

Let it Go

One of the signature moments of "Frozen," is when Elsa sings "Let It Go." The basic premise of this now infamous song is to let go of everything that is holding you back. Sounds like a powerful message to me. In fact, I would argue that in the movie it was at this moment when Elsa realized that she doesn't need to run or hide anymore, and that she can "let go" of everything that is holding her back and start to be proud of who she really is. So again yes I completely understand that "Frozen" is a kid's animated movie that is rated G, but I would also argue that this doesn't mean that as adults we can't relate to what Elsa had to go through. We all go through certain points in our life where we're faced with certain choices. We all have these reflection points or crossroads where we have to decide if we're going to make real changes and let go of all our bullshit, or keep doing what we're doing and remain feeling stuck.

I know this is a very hard process. As a culture, we're consumed with anger and judgment. A lot of our anger and frustration is rightly justified. From social injustice and oppression, to the way some of us were treated, and to environmental factors as well, there are many valid reasons as to why we have so much inner rage. So for me to suggest that you just need to "Let it Go," and move on from all the anger, and hurt and pain that you've experienced for years seems not only disingenuous, but reinforces your initial thought that I'm living in this fairy tale world. Just keep reading.

For me, a lot my anger stems from racism that I experienced

in middle school and especially high school. From racial slurs, to racial gestures (people slanting their eyes to mimic my facial features), and to racial stereotypes, being Asian was thrown in my face for the majority of my adolescence. I was made to feel inferior for being Asian. Now I do want to note that yes I felt targeted because the color of my skin and my physical features, but thankfully I was never subjected to physical violence. If that has happened to you or someone you love I am not suggesting that you "Let it go," or move on. If this is your situation than that's a different story, and my hope is that you get the help and support you need to start healing from your trauma. Things need to change in this country from police reform, to how we treat one another, to especially who we elect and put in public office. But is it possible for me to basically start over and let go of all the anger and pain that has consumed me since I was a teenager? My answer to this question is simply, I have too. I have to learn how to let go of all this shit so I can finally move on with my life. This starts by going back to the basics and allow myself to just love who I am.

Think back to when you were kid. Can you remember the times when you were just happy and care-free? Do you remember when you weren't influenced by other people? Can you remember when you went to bed happy and were actually excited to wake up the next day because you loved life so much? Now can you remember when things started to change and you started to internalize the message you were receiving from society, your peers, and your community? One of the more difficult parts of parenting is when parents start to lose the messaging battle. Many parents really struggle with this and start to feel helpless when their kid starts to become more consumed and persuaded by the messages coming from their peers and society. Parents will tell their kids that they're special and that they're beautiful just the way they are. Society and peers come along and say that's actually not true, and that you're overweight, ugly, and don't belong here. This is what makes it extremely difficult for anyone to really love themselves. We not only focus on our faults and what we don't like about ourselves, but messages we receive from society and our peers not only get embedded inside of us, but they start to define how we feel about ourselves. I'm not saying that this will be easy. The things that we carry have a lot weight to them. From the time we wake up to the time we fall asleep we spend more time and more energy focusing on our faults and inadequacies and what we don't like about ourselves. Start the process of getting to know yourself again. Focus on your successes and the things that you're really proud of. Push yourself to make changes, but give yourself credit along the way. Words can also hurt, and people can tear us down. Let it go and start the process of loving yourself again. I don't know about you, but for me I'm done with letting other people determine how I feel about myself. The time is now to let it go and be done with all the crap that has defined you for years.

Embrace Who You Are

Embracing who you are will require you to do two things. First, stop running from your problems. In the movie "Frozen," Elsa ran from her problems and escaped by going up to the mountains. It's easy to run from our problems, it's even easier to blame other people for our own failures and for how we feel. Now part of the process of embracing who you are will also require you to go deep and ask yourself some very tough questions. You're at a crossroads right now, either you can run, or you can make some very tough decisions. Stop running. The easy thing to do is to dismiss what I'm saying and keep running. You're going to tell yourself that "I'm wrong and that I don't know what I'm talking about." That's the definition of running. I know this is hard. I ran for years and directed all my anger and confusion towards my parents. Now my wife gets the brunt of my issues. Stop running and deal with your problems. Change is never easy, especially looking inward and asking yourself some very hard questions.

We all have certain judgements and biases. No one is perfect especially not me. Either you can start to process your own faults and preconceptions, or keeping going to your safe corner and continue blaming other people for your problems. If you do this and retreat to your safe side where people reinforce that other people are the problem, I wouldn't judge you for it and quite honestly I really do get it. Again, change is hard and change is uncomfortable. At the same time if you don't address your faults and your biases you're going to keep coming to these crossroads throughout your life. Part of Elsa's journey was to stop running, face her problems, and embrace who she is. That's what I'm asking you to do. Face your problems without blaming other people, and work towards positive change. So you have a choice. Either you can embrace the fact that you're bitter, angry, and mean; or you can embrace that fact that you need to make some serious changes. Do you need to work on being more patient and being less judgmental? What about being more empathic and more caring towards other people? Whatever your case may be let this be the time that you finally stop running and move towards real change.

Number 2, self-acceptance. One of the main story plots of "Frozen," is Elsa's path towards self-acceptance. Elsa not only had to accept the fact that she was different, but also be able to embrace her differences. The positive message of this movie is that if you embrace who you are, you can then overcome any obstacle that is in your way. For Elsa, she had to not only embrace her majestic powers, but also stop running from her problems and own up to her mistakes. Part of self-acceptance is the ability to accept every part of you, even the parts that you despise and are ashamed of. Self-acceptance is a very difficult concept. What we try to do is either hide or mask the parts of us that we don't like. We either avoid or suppress the emotions that are either too painful or to confusing.

Growing up one of my favorite movies that I would watch with my sister was "Pretty in Pink." The main character (Andie), played by Molly Ringwald tried to hide and run from the fact that she was poor, and didn't come from money like some of her peers. Like Elsa, Molly Ringwald's character not only had to stop running, but also stand up to those who were putting her down, and be proud of who she is. Could Andie embrace the fact that she was poor? Probably not, and that's not what I'm suggesting you do either if right now you are in living in poverty or less than ideal circumstances. Asking you to do something like that is extremely insensitive. What I do believe is that despite your socioeconomic status you don't have to be ashamed of yourself. That's the part of you that you need to let go of so that you can start to live a better life.

The opposite of self-acceptance is self-loathing. This is what we're really good at. In fact, for a lot of us this comes as second nature. We only pay attention to our inadequacies or the things that we just don't like about ourselves. The thing about self-loathing is that this is an immensely powerful force. Self-loathing is so powerful that it can take us to very dark places both in regards to self-harm and also hatred towards others. To me hate is only a reflection of how we truly feel about ourselves. Now I'm not trying to imply that you're a racist or an extremist or anything like that. What I am trying to imply is that self-loathing will manifest itself in one of two ways. Either you are going to hate yourself or you are going to direct your self-loathing towards other people. Whichever way self-loathing reveals itself, neither is good and both will prevent you from getting to where you want to be in life. The point here is for you to be self-aware of when you are feeling self-loathing so that you can make changes and be able to work on loving yourself again and embracing who you are.

So what we're going to do is start embracing who we really are. No more running. I'll go first. My name is Justin. I'm a 40 year old Asian male, father of two incredible boys. I'm adopted from Korea, and have a white family. This is what I've tried to hide for the majority of my life, but yet this is who I am. No more hiding. I drive a car that no one in their right mind would ever want to steal so I rarely, if ever remember to lock the doors. I pledge to myself that I will stop running from my problems and strive towards letting go of all the anger and resentment that is in my heart. I believe in equality and human rights, and also believe that it is our obligation and responsibility to protect and conserve this environment for future generations. My name is Justin and this is who I am.

That actually felt really good. Now it's your turn. Say it with me. I'm _____, and this is who I am. I'm not going to let my appearance, my mental health, my upbringing, or society weigh me down any longer. I'm going to embrace who I am. Feels good doesn't it? No more running. No more hiding.

Start Trusting Other People

The last part of Elsa's journey was for her to start trusting other people again. Elsa had to come to the decision to start letting other people back in her life, and get to a place where she could start believing in the human spirit again. Like Elsa, this process won't be easy. It's human nature to be cautious of other people, and also to have your guard up. We live in a different time right now where it's now unsafe to let your child walk to school. Shit if you're not careful enough and if you trust the wrong person or open up the wrong email than you're identity gets taken from you. As a culture we hurt each other, let each other down, betray each other's trust, and spread gossip about one another on the internet. The issue here is that if we don't allow other people in and if we don't allow ourselves to start trusting people again we will inevitably end up alone. I can't promise you that this will be easy, because it won't especially if you've been really hurt or if you've been violated by other people. What I can promise you is that if you want to get better than on some level you have to start trusting other people again.

So how do we this? Let's start by giving other people a chance. So what does that mean? If you want to start the process of trusting other people again this begins by allowing other people to show you who they truly are and that they can be trusted. What I don't want is for you to have the mindset that people need to pass a test in order for you to start trusting them. If you have this mindset of pass or fail, than no one will ever be able to pass your test because no one is perfect. You can however, give people a chance and start opening yourself up one small crack at a time. I'm not expecting nor do I want you to tell everyone you meet everything about you. What you'll need to do is pick and choose what you want to share and with who, and also what you feel comfortable disclosing. This of course is different if you're in an intimate relationship that starts to get serious. If this is the case you'll need to take the risk and really start to allow the other person to help comfort and soothe your insecurities and emotional wounds. Elsa started this process by letting her sister Anna back in her life. Start slow, but give people a chance. Regardless of your history this process is hard. The fear of rejection, the possibility of being let down are all very real outcomes that will most likely happen from time to time. The thing here is that the process of trusting other people is like a cycle. It's hard at first, but trusts me it gets easier. It was hard for Elsa, just like it was hard for me, as it will be for you as well. It does get easier, and the more you start trusting other people the more you will be able to tolerate and accept moments of rejection and disappointment.

Next, treat human relationships the same way you do or you

would with your pets. As humans we treat our animals very differently than we do other people. Let me acknowledge that pets/ animals are safer than people, but just like people, pets also let us down. Ever come home from work and your dog either chews up your favorite pair of shoes, or has an accident inside your home? At first you're really upset and overreact, but as soon as your pet gives you that look you quickly forgive and forget. We treat animals very differently than we treat humans. Elsa had Olaf. In most cases we either have a cat(s) or dog(s). The point here is that with people we hold grudges, but when it comes to our pets we're much more patient and accepting of their behavior and mistakes. What we can start to do is learn how to transition our trust and patience with our pets, to real life other people. Yes, I know this will be hard and I fully understand that pets typically don't hurt us on the same level as humans do. What I also believe is that you don't need to hide who you are. You can be your authentic self around other people, just like how you are around your pet.

Your pet has your entire heart. There's nothing you wouldn't do or give to your pet. Your animal is your entire world. I never understood dog people. My view was that whichever way you view it at the end of the day they're still a dog. I didn't get it, until my wife and I got our own dog. Now I get it. I couldn't write this book without acknowledging my dog C.C. My wife has a side joke with our friends and family about how C.C. is my mistress. I truly believe that C.C. has not only helped me let other people in, but has really helped my two boys open up to people as well. Pets bring out the best in us. Now use this to your advantage as you start the process of trusting other people again.

Lastly, stay with it. Be consistent, roll with the punches, but don't give up. In EMDR therapy we have this saying of "trust the process." That's what I'm going to ask you to do "trust the process." Remember it's easy to run. I ran for years and was always skeptical of other people. Challenge yourself to see the best in other people, and begin the process of starting to trust other people again. I promise you the more you do this the more it will get easier for you. You'll just need to take the risk and start putting yourself out there.

CHAPTER 7
FAITH

I SAVED FAITH and religion for the last chapter on purpose. If you've made it this far than just hear me out. Let me first just acknowledge that yes, religion is a very sensitive topic. I'm going to ask you to just stay with me and try to keep an open mind to what I'm saying. I'm not a pastor, nor do I have a theology degree so therefore throughout this chapter I will stay in my lane and not preach to you. What I would like to do is try to make a rule and agree on something simple. Let's make an agreement, I won't judge you if you don't judge me. Whether you lost faith, never had faith, or if your faith is strong and secure, let's agree that no matter where you are in life name calling and passing judgement on one another just doesn't help. I'll talk sides in just a couple of moments, but before I do that let me address the name calling and the labels that we place on each other.

Both sides do it, and my thought is that if you don't like being placed in a certain category or box then don't do it to the other group. As a therapist, I have never believed in putting people in certain categories or giving them labels. For example, if you label a kid as a "bad kid," then guess what you're going to get- a bad kid. If you give them a more positive and humane label then you'll get a different response.

It's the same thing with religion. The religious community labels people who don't believe the way they believe or think the way they think as either non-believers or even worse, as sinners. If you don't have faith you label those who do as either crazy or view them as "there's just something wrong with those people." Now, regardless of what side you're on you may be saying to yourself "well I think that way because I'm right." If you have this mentality or if you have this perspective that my view is right, theirs is wrong, than what do you think that says about you? Why do you feel more comfortable judging someone rather than listening to them? What does it say about you that you're more comfortable with disapproving of other people's lifestyles and their views, instead of being more tolerant and open-minded?

So maybe by now you're in full disagreement with me. If you're down in life what do you think would motivate you? Someone who encourages you, motivates you, and lifts you up or someone who dismisses your hurt and pain and shames you for having those feelings? If your goal right now is to lead other people to Christ, then start by acknowledging their hurt and pain. Be an example of compassion and understanding. Things like discrimination, poverty, systemic racism, and oppression still exist in our society. Instead of just trying to pray away things like hate and violence, listen to the fears and anxieties people have about our current climate.

Secondly, let's try to agree that sometimes life can feel upside down. The simple truth is that life is hard. Life brings pain and obstacles that we have to face. It's taken me a lifetime to understand that God can't just simply take away all my hurt and pain. What faith has done for me is given me hope and direction. God may not be able to take away all the confusion and disappointment I have, but what He has done is given me an internal compass and morals and values to live by. Every single one of us moves through the same life transitions from infancy to late adulthood. Some people handle difficult life transitions (i.e. adolescents and middle adulthood) better than others, but in general we all struggle getting older. It's part of life, but before you tell someone that you'll pray for them when the majority of you say one prayer and then never think about that person ever again, just be there for them and support them. Is prayer important? Yes, of course it is, but so is validating their pain and struggle.

When I was growing up and would share my inner personal struggles with the parish staff where I went to church they would constantly tell me "everything happens for a reason." Or I would constantly hear "God will take care of it." I acknowledge that God has gotten me through some very difficult and challenging times in my life. However, for someone to say "everything happens for a reason," is not only a disingenuous response, but also insincere and insensitive as well. In fact, you might be saying to yourself, "I wonder what the other person thinks to themselves when I say to them 'everything happens for a reason?' Well I'll tell you, we think to ourselves, OK asshole, why don't you try and live my life for just two seconds and then come back to me and tell me if you still think "everything happens for a reason." Pain and suffering are real. Prayer helps, but first meet people where they are at and acknowledge that life can often feel impossible.

Lastly, regardless of what you believe, let's try and agree that there are good people on both sides. If you don't have faith, focus on the people and the community leaders who are doing the right thing. It's easy to focus on and get turned off by the televangelists who make a profit off people's suffering and misfortune. Or, the TV pastor who at the time when his community needed him the most (i.e. Hurricane Harvey) turned his back on his community instead of opening up his mega church to people in need. It was only after getting negative media attention did he then proclaim that his church is open to all those in need. If you solely focus on these people your view of faith and religion will always be skewed. However, there are religious figures that put the needs of their congregation well before their own needs. There are pastoral leaders who take on the role and the responsibility to be an activist in their community, pillars of hope and change, and speak the true word of God. Let these leaders and religious figures be the image you think of when you think of religion. Don't allow the fake pastors who place money and fame before the word of God twist your view of religion.

The same goes to all of you who have faith. Just because someone doesn't have faith doesn't mean they are a bad person. Can people be very cynical and immoral? Of course, but that doesn't mean that everyone who lacks faith is evil. My thought is that you allow past experiences to pre-determine how you view someone who does not share the same beliefs that you do. Think about it for a second. Ever had a spiritual debate with someone who you just couldn't get through to? What happens is the next time you have a spiritual debate you not only remember this interaction and how frustrating this was for you, but you look for things that reinforce your view about non-believers. Pretty soon your perception about the other side is set in stone. If your goal is to really be the light at the top of the hill and lead people to Christ, then you have nothing but my utmost praise and admiration. Isn't our goal as Christians, is to make a positive impact on the world by being an example of love and acceptance? Be patient with people, and plant seeds of hope and encouragement. Let the part of you that is judgmental and disapproving drop, and instead allow the part of you that is open-minded to come out.

Tune out the Noise

Part of reclaiming your faith will require you to tune out the noise. Let me give you an example. Ever turned on the news and watched a cable news correspondent who represents the religious right go on a show and talk about complete nonsense? Ever been really turned off by how they conduct themselves and what they say? I have. Even worse, ever seen some nutjob use their platform to promote hate and fear, but hide behind the fact that they are claiming to speak the word of God? Believe me they are not speaking truth. They are only fake pastors who are only tearing apart an already divided country. So tune out the noise and allow yourself to press reset.

Despite what other people say there are countless reasons why someone either struggles with their faith or walks away from the church. Notice how I didn't say loses their faith, but struggles with their faith. I'll get into that in just a second, but let me first talk about my own family of origin.

Religion played a central role in my life growing up, but it also played a key role in tearing my family apart as well. In my own development I struggled off and on with faith and have questioned where God was during the most painful and confusing times of my life. Does this mean that I am less of a Christian than you? Does this mean that your God loves you more than me? If you think the answer to these questions is yes, then my encouragement to you is to read James 4:11-12, or Romans 3:23, and then get back to me. Just because you either lack faith or have walked away from the church does not mean that you are a bad person. Again, religion caused a huge rift in my family and ultimately some of my siblings to this day don't go to church. If you asked them they would probably cite a lot of different reasons as to why they stopped going to church. However, I believe one of the main reasons why they stopped going to church was that the message no longer spoke to them. In actuality, I truly feel that religious leaders need to take a look at this. What is the message that their congregation is hearing? Is it a message that promotes hope and encouragement? Or is the message based off of negativity and fear? You're not giving enough, you're not thinking the right way, you're not acting the way you should. People go to church to feel inspired. We want to feel hopeful. We want to feel connected to the congregation. If the church's message is consistently a scare tactic then why would someone keep going to church? I know the things that I'm doing wrong in my life. What I need is to feel motivated and inspired. What I don't need is to be reminded of how much of a piece of shit I am. Believe me, I think that way enough about myself throughout the day.

If you feel this way and if you have taken a break from the church, listen to me carefully. You are not a bad person. In fact, I believe you are more of a Christian than those who go to church only out of obligation. Give those people a quiz after church and they have no idea what was said, what the message was, or what the readings were about. What they can tell you is what their Monday is going to look like, and what they have planned throughout the week. Well at least I go to church. Yes you go to church, but you only go through the motions. Stand when you're supposed to stand, kneel when you're supposed to kneel, and come Monday morning you're back to being a dick. My guess is that if it was allowed you would probably be on your phone during church posting shit on social media. My hope for you and my encouragement for my own family are to do four things.

First, again tune out the noise and press reset. Faith is inside you whether you know it or not. I told you before I started this chapter that I will not preach to you. Remember? I'm going to keep my word, but trust me faith is inside you whether you feel it or not. Want proof? Ever passed by someone and had this sudden rush of compassion for that person? Maybe they were homeless, or had a disability, or you just felt that they were hurting inside. That's faith. Ever had a feeling that despite everything around you was falling apart that you were still going to be OK? That's also faith.

Second, reopen the dialogue with God. I don't care if you talk with Him while you're driving to work or in the grocery store. The point here is to just start talking. I fully understand that for some of you this will be really difficult and also scary for you as well. Will God really listen? Does He really forgive me? Does He really understand my pain? Does He even care about me anymore? Those are all very real feelings and valid questions. I go back to this, just start talking to God and see what happens. While we are on it let me quickly address pain and suffering. I personally don't think that there is a reasonable explanation as to why there is so much pain and suffering in the world. I'm sure there are some nut cases out there that have an explanation as to why bad shit happens to good people, and if you really want to I'm sure you can find them on the internet and see what they have to say. For me, I won't pretend to know or explain why some people had to experience some of the things they were subjected to. In fact, religion sends a very different confusing message when it comes to pain and trauma. Ever heard this saying before, "you have to forgive those who have hurt you?" I promise there are some of you reading this right now who are really struggling with the concept of forgiveness. From a young age we are told to forgive others. The concept of forgiveness is engrained in our heads at an early age and if we either can't or just don't want to forgive we feel even worse about ourselves. So here's my theory about forgiveness. Yes it is a very powerful and also important concept. However, forgiveness is also this very loaded word that is thrown around in our culture. People preach forgiveness, "turn the other cheek and love your enemies." You know what the majority of us do? We just move on with our lives. But guess what? That's not forgiveness. So for those who sit there and preach forgiveness let me ask who have you really forgiven?

In graduate school I learned about Lawrence Kohlberg's stages of moral development. Kohlberg theorized that only around 10 to 15 percent of the population will actually make it to the last stage of morality, "post-conventional morality." (Vinney, 2019). To make it to this final stage of morality, people will need to have a level of abstract reasoning. During graduate school, it was discussed that the majority of us fall into the second stage of moral development "Conventional Mortality," with a very small percentage of the population who actually make it to the final stage of Post-conventional Morality. If you are really in the last stage of moral development then you are in the company of people like Mother Teresa and your behavior and character are congruent with your values of forgiveness and selflessness. If you have really made it to this level of morality then feel free to tweet at me. For the rest of us, including myself, we should all be striving to get to this last stage of morality. However, why judge someone who is suffering and even worse judge them for not doing something that you can't do yourself (i.e. practice forgiveness).

Want an example? Let's say someone enters your congregation seeking compassion and forgiveness. It happens all the time, right? At the same time, the community knows that this person has committed blasphemy. Just FYI, I could have used someone having an abortion for this example, but if I did that I would be worried that people would burn my book. Anyways, back to the example. If you knew this person was really seeking redemption and healing would you offer forgiveness or pass judgement on this person? If this scenario happened would your automatic thought be judgement or forgiveness? If it's really forgiveness then change the sin and do the exercise again. The point here is that we are all sinful in nature. At the same time, most of us are doing the best we can and are striving towards being able to forgive. Reopen your dialogue with God and don't let anyone deter or affect your relationship with Christ.

Third, open up your ears. Start listening to Christian music. We all listen to music. In fact, music plays such a large role in our lives. From Spotify, to ITunes, to Pandora and Amazon, music is as popular now as it ever has been. When we need it the most, music speaks to us, it motivates us, and helps us get through the day. Angry about a recent break-up? Listen to some Taylor Swift or play some 80's music. Wanna get hyped up for a workout, or a big game? Listen to some rap music or heavy metal.

My argument here is give Christian music a chance. Let God speak to you through Christian music. I can't tell you how many times the right song played, at the right moment just when I needed it the most. Christian music has literally brought me to my knees. It's at these moments when I believe God is telling me "I got you." On some level we all do this. We allow music to help reset us and balance us out. Had a tough day at work? What do you do on your drive home? You change the radio until you find that perfect song that really speaks to you, and calms you down. Think back to when you were a kid, and your parents would tell you "why do you listen to that type of music?" Yes you liked the beat and rhythm of your music and the artist as well, but the reason we are drawn to music so much is that it speaks to us. Music understands us. It gets us, and doesn't judge us. Music understands the pain and confusion we feel on a daily basis.

Give Christian music a chance. Get to know some of the artist and their personal stories, and how God influenced their life. I think for some people, they have this mentality that Christians don't know what true pain and misery feel like. They have this perfect life so why I would listen to anything they have to say? Let me just say, you're probably right. There are a lot of people in this country, Christian and non-Christian alike that live inside this perfect bubble and are oblivious to the pain and suffering that people feel around this world.

There are however, Christians like Mandisa. Now if you know who Mandisa is, you probably know that she's a past contestant on American Idol. You also might know that she is a grammy award winning gospel singer. What you might not know is that back in 2014 after her best friend died, she went into a major depression where she isolated herself from friends and family, gained over 200 lbs, and even contemplated suicide (Nelson, 2020). I don't know about you, but that sounds like a very real person to me. It also sounds like God really helped Mandisa get through one of the darkest moments in her life.

There's also Kirk Franklin. From the outside looking in you might think to yourself that Kirk has everything anybody could have ever wanted. A beautiful family, fame and wealth, a prestigious career, and not to mention being named in People's Magazine as one of the sexiest men alive. Along with adding 15 time grammy award winning artist to Kirk Franklin's title, you can also add overcomer as well. Since being 8 years old, Kirk struggled with a serious pornography addiction that affected his marriage, his self-worth, his faith, and his career (Oprah.com, 2005). Kirk was able to overcome his addiction with the love of his wife, support from his community, and a renewed faith in God (Oprah.com, 2005). The point here is that everyone has their problems, and whether you're famous or not, God can change your life and help you get back on track. Give Christian music a chance. Open up your ears and allow God to speak to you through artist like Mandisa and Kirk Franklin. I promise you if you give Christian music a chance you'll feel God telling you "I got you."

Lastly, go back to church. Try different churches, feel out different congregations, but start going back to church. If this book is all about finding happiness and direction in your life then my hope for you is that you either give religion a chance, or you recommit yourself to a life of faith. Remember faith is in you, whether you know it or not.

CHAPTER 8
CONCLUSION

THROUGHOUT THIS BOOK my quest was to figure out what separates those who are truly happy from those who aren't. Different people will have different reasons for the root cause of unhappiness from biology, to family of origin, to socio-economic status. While all of these factors are legitimate reasons for someone's happiness or unhappiness, the truth of the matter is that we all have to live our lives and get through this thing called life.

Now, do things need to change in our society? Yes absolutely, and it starts with equality. I completely understand that the opportunity and the prosperity that my kids are going to have will look very different from other kids around this country. From family dynamics, to their community, to the schools they attend, their life will look a lot different from other kids. That's not to say I should be ashamed of this, because I'm not, but the disparity in this county needs to change. Until the day comes where everyone and every kid gets the equal chance to succeed, it's our job to support one another. So what does support mean? True support for those who are struggling starts with lifting them up. Imagine that you're really struggling right now and you're really down in life. Now take that same feeling, but imagine knowing and feeling that your community was behind you. Imagine if you truly felt that people cared for you and were in your corner. Now imagine how much easier it would be to take on life challenges with the support of other people.

I promise you one common thread that separates happy people from those who are angry and resentful is a strong support system. Support is like a cycle. By supporting people in a selfless manner, you get support back when you need it the most. So let's say you take the risk and put yourself out there for a job promotion, which is what very happy and content people do. They put themselves out there and take risks in life knowing that sometimes they might fail. Does having self-confidence help when it comes to taking risks? Sure it does. You know what else helps? A really good support system. Taking risks in life is easier said than done especially when it comes to the possibility of rejection. Nobody wants to ask someone out on a date or prepare for a job interview only to face the possibility of rejection and humiliation. If however, you have a solid support system in place taking risks in life just comes easier. Start putting yourself out there and build up your support system with people who will accept you unconditionally.

The issue here is that life won't wait for us. The opportunities of today aren't guaranteed to be here tomorrow. It is up to us to learn how to take risks and put ourselves out there. Yes, we might fail, but with failure comes opportunity. Opportunity to not only reinvent ourselves, but also allow ourselves to press reset and start over. We all have a certain amount of anxiety about our life and about the future. What we can learn from previous generations is that if we expect life to wait for us then we are bound to be disappointed. Life moves at such a rapid pace. In order to keep up with this ever-changing world we have to constantly adapt and also push ourselves both personally, professionally, and spiritually.

If the pain and hurt of past experiences have caused you to be resentful and angry, then push yourself to do something different and start by changing your cognition. As we develop and grow, certain things start to become engrained in our minds. From what we can and can't do, to how we feel about ourselves. Our challenge is to push all the negative beliefs out and allow positive beliefs to grow. Know that with any sort of change the more you do something over and over the more it becomes second nature. Start incorporating self-soothing skills into your daily routine. Allow deep breathing to balance your emotions and relax your body.

After your mind and body feel balanced and centered, accept the challenge and start seeing the good in other people. What we often do is see what we want to see in other people and focus on their shortcomings. Take the risk and start seeing the good in other people. Will this be hard? Absolutely, it's human nature to be skeptical of other people. We judge people based on how they look, their appearance, their social class, and their demeanor. Are there times when people's affect will match our pre-conceived notion of them? Sure, without a doubt. My guess is that if you really think about it there are probably more times than not that we've misjudged people based on our initial impression of them. Once we started to get to know that person we quickly found out that our judgement about them was wrong. Are there people in our culture that abuse their power and take advantage of the position they have? Unfortunately, yes. Does this need to change immediately starting with holding people accountable? Absolutely, yes. The point here is that we can alter what we want to see in other people, while at the same time change how we come across to other people as well.

One of the harder challenges we face is to look inwards and change or adjust how other people see us. Will some people get it wrong and misjudge you? Sure, this might happen. However, most people have an idea about who they want to be around, or who they want to hire. People can feel and distinguish between someone who is approachable and who is open-minded from those who are closed off, angry, and shallow minded. How we present ourselves to other people will have lasting consequences that can be both positive and negative. If you walk around all the time with a chip on your shoulder you are bound to repel people and live a life of isolation and despair. Now other people may try and change you, but the real change needs to come from within. Challenge yourself and take the risk of always presenting the best part of you.

Finally, reopen your dialogue with God. Religion is a lot like politics. It just turns a lot of people off. I will openly admit that it would be very easy to use the current political environment as a reason to walk away from religion. This is really just one of the reasons why some people decide to stop going to church. Regardless of why you stopped going to church, my encouragement to you is to not allow other people to dictate your faith. Reopen your dialogue with God. Start to have faith for yourself and allow God to direct your life. There are several reasons why someone may have given up on religion, but I believe faith can positively change our lives for the better. I wish I had a rational explanation or could explain why some people have to go through the things they do in life. I wish I had a logical explanation as to why some people especially kids get things like cancer and terminal illnesses, but I don't. What I can tell you is that I have sat with people and been with them during their finals days. I've sat in amazement and marveled at their courage and their faith as well. I left feeling inspired that despite going through the impossible and knowing that the end was inevitable their character never changed. I don't know about you, but for me I believe I owe it to them to always try and improve myself on a daily basis. I owe it to them to do away with all the malice and judgement in my heart. I owe it to my kids to be a better example of compassion, patience, and empathy towards others. Yes life can be hard and it can feel impossible at times. Life can present some challenges, but life can also be what we want it to be as well.

So congratulations for choosing to improve your life. Start with writing down goals and then identify the following steps that you will need to do in order to accomplish your goals. Regardless of whether your goal is a personal goal of establishing sobriety or losing weight, or a professional goal of getting a new job, come up with a treatment plan as to how you are going to accomplish your goals. Challenge yourself to not give up despite what roadblocks may come up. Push yourself to go beyond your limits. Wishing you peace and happiness.

REFERENCES

Abcarian, R. (2016, July). Michelle Obama's stunning convention speech: 'When they go low, we go high.' *Los Angeles Times.* Retrieved from https://www.latimes.com/politics/la-na-pol-michelle-speech-20160725-snap-story.html

Amthor, F. (2012). *Neuroscience for Dummiers.* John Wiley & Sons Canada, Ltd.

Apatow, J., & Miller, J. (Producer), & McKay, A. (Director). (2006). *Talledega Nights: The Ballad of Ricky Bobby* [Motion Picture]. United States: Columbia Pictures.

Bailey, R. (2019, July). Amygdala's Location and Function Fear and the Amygdala. *ThoughtCo.* Retrieved from https://www.thoughtco.com/amygdala-anatomy-373211

Bender, L. (Producer), & Van Sant, G. (Director). (1997). Good Will Hunting [Motion Picture]. United States: Miramax.

Carter, C. (2017, November). How to Cope with a Difficult Relative Over the Holidays. Retrieved from URL https://www.

christinecarter.com/2017/11/how-to-cope-with-a-difficult
-relative-over-the-holidays

Carter, R. (2010). *Mapping the Mind*. University of California Press.

Cherry, K. (2020, April). Left brain vs. Right brain is the analytical-creative separation true or false? *Verywell Mind*. Retrieved from https://www.verywellmind.com/left-brain-vs-right-brain-2795005

Davis, K. (2020, June). Everything you need to know about cannabis. *Medical News Today*. Retrieved from https://www.medicalnewstoday.com/articles/246392

Del Vecho, P. (Producer), & Buck, C., & Lee, J. (Directors). (2013). Frozen [Motion Picture]. United States: Walt Disney Animation Studios

DiSalvo, D. (2012, October). What Alcohol Really does to Your Brain. *Forbes Magazine*. Retrieved from https://www.forbes.com/sites/daviddisalvo/2012/10/16/what-alcohol-really-does-to-your-brain/#5027dcb1664e

Effects of Alcohol. (2019). Retrieved from URL https://alcoholaddictioncenter.org/alcohol/effects/

Elkins, K. (2015, May). From poverty to a $3 billion fortune- the incredible rags-to-riches story of Oprah Winfrey. *Business Insider*. Retrieved from https://www.businessinsider.com/rags-to-riches-story-of-oprah-winfrey-2015-5

Greenberg, M. (2017, April). Stuck in Negative Thinking? It could be your brain. *Psychology Today*. Retrieved from https://www.psychologytoday.com/us/blog/the-mindful-self-express/201704/stuck-in-negative-thinking-it-could-be-your-brain

Jio, S. (2009, November). Guess the day of the week when most people call in sick. *Glamour Magazine*. Retrieved from https://www.glamour.com/story/guess-the-day-of-the-week-when

Kinberg, S. (Producer), & Miller, T. (Director). (2016). *Deadpool* [Motion Picture]. Canada: 20th Century Fox.

Knappenberger, B. (Director), & Parke S., Hermann, J., Palmour, C., Temple, J., & Therolf, G. (Producers). (2020). *The trials of Gabriel Fernandez*. [TV mini-series]. Retrieved from http://www.netflix.com/

Landin-Romero R., Kumfor F., Leyton, CE, Irish M., Hodges, JR, & Piguet O. (2016). Disease specific patterns, of cortical and subcortical degeneration in a longitudinal study of Alzheimer's disease and behavioural-variant frontotemporal dementia. *Neuorimage*, 151, 72-80. Retrieved from https://pubmed.ncbi.nlm.nih.gov/27012504/

Larsen, C. (2016, August). Using EMDR to Find your 'safe place' in Trauma Recovery. *GoodTherapy*. Retrieved from https://www.goodtherapy.org/blog/using-emdr-to-find-your-safe-place-in-trauma-recovery-0815164

Lowenthal, T. (2015, July). How to set clear-cut boundaries in dysfunctional family relationships. *About Redlands Network*. Retrieved from URL https://aboutredlands.com/articles/

how-to-set-clear-cut-boundaries-in-dysfunctional-family-relationships

Nelson, J. (2017, May). American Idol's Mandisa was suicidal, gained 200 lbs. after her friend's death: 'I'm still here' after feeling 'so hopeless.' *People Magazine*. Retrieved from https://people.com/music/mandisa-suicidal-depression-weight-gain-after-friends-death/

Pierre-Bravo, D. (2017, November). John Paul DeJoria's journey from homeless to billionaire. *NBC News*. Retrieved from https://www.nbcnews.com/know-your-value/feature/john-paul-dejoria-s-journey-homeless-billionaire-ncna825246

Porn Epidemic. (2005, November). *Oprah.com*. Retrieved from https://www.oprah.com/oprahshow/porn-epidemic/all

Riopel, L. (2020, April). The importance, benefits, and value of goal setting. *Positive Psychology*. Retrieved from https://positivepsychology.com/benefits-goal-setting/

Sackey, C. (2017, December). From Rags to Riches: The story of Oprah Winfrey. *STMU History Media*. Retrieved from https://stmuhistorymedia.org/from-rags-to-riches-the-story-of-oprah-winfrey/

Santhanam, L. (2019, October). Youth suicide rates are on the rise in the U.S. PBS News Hour. Retrieved from https://www.pbs.org/newshour/health/youth-suicide-rates-are-on-the-rise-in-the-u-s

Shuler Donner, L. (Producer), & Deutch, H. (Director). (1986). Pretty in Pink [Motion Picture]. United States: Paramount Pictures.

Shapiro, F. (2018). *Eye Movement Desensitization and Reprocessing (EMDR) Therapy Basic Principles, Protocols, and Procedures Third Edition.* The Guilford Press.

Trudeau, M. (2010, January). Teen Drinking May Cause Irreversible Brain Damage. *Your Health.* Retrieved from URL https://www.npr.org/templates/story/story.php?storyId=122765890

Vinney, C. (2019, June). Kohlberg Stages of Moral Development. Retrieved from URL https://www.thoughtco.com/kohlbergs-stages-of-moral-development-4689125

Weiner Davis, M. (2001). *The Divorce Remedy The proven 7-step program for saving your marriage.* Simon & Schuster Paperbacks.

80 Powerful Affirmations that could change your life. (2019, January). *Mindvalley.* Retrieved from https://blog.mindvalley.com/positive-affirmations/

85% of People Hate Their Jobs, Gallup Poll says. (2017, September). *Return to Now.* Retrieved from URL https://returntonow.net/2017/09/22/85-people-hate-jobs-gallup-poll-says/

Printed in the United States
By Bookmasters